COURAGE

CAN CHANGE

Finding Your Path: The Role of Courage in Personal Reinvention

By

JAYAA MISHRA

DEDICATION

This book is dedicated to my beloved mother

KUSUM

WHY SHOULD YOU READ THIS BOOK?

Success in any area of life—whether professional, personal, or relational—requires one essential quality: courage.

The most successful people in the world stand out because they possess the courage to make decisions and take bold actions toward their dreams.

They are clear about what they want in life and are fearless in pursuing it, regardless of the challenges they face. This clarity and bravery propel them to the top.

On the other hand, living a life dominated by fear holds us back. When we constantly question -

"What if this goes wrong?" or

"What if that doesn't happen?"

We allow fear to dictate our choices. This fear keeps us stuck in mediocrity, preventing us from envisioning and striving for a better life.

Courage is the driving force that enables us to move forward, overcome obstacles, and achieve our dreams. It empowers us to rise above our doubts and take the necessary steps to transform our lives.

This book will guide you to understand and confront your fears, providing practical insights and strategies to help you cultivate courage. By taking those first brave steps, you too can achieve your goals and create the life you've always dreamed of. It's time to embrace courage and unlock your potential for success.

PREAMBLE

"Courage Can Change" is a testament to the transformative power of courage in reshaping personal and professional lives. It explores how even the most minor steps taken for one's well-being can be acts of immense bravery. This book delves deep into the struggles, breakthroughs, and ultimate triumphs of daring to change one's life narrative. It is a story and a journey of self-discovery, self-love, and the unshakeable power of saying "Yes" to oneself.

Growing up, I faced relentless rejection and discrimination, especially for something as superficial as skin color. In my childhood, the conditioning was simple yet suffocating: whatever the elders said was final. You couldn't question them, let alone defy them. This left me with a deeply ingrained fear of confrontation. I became a people-pleaser, constantly seeking approval, often at the cost of my happiness and self-worth. My low self-esteem made me quiet and fearful, unable to advocate for myself.

When I got married, the same pattern continued. In a household where tradition held sway, I silently complied with my in-laws' demands, doing everything they asked. Balancing a full-time job with house chores, I endured taunts and criticism from my mother-in-law and sister-in-law, all while burying my feelings and desires. Fear dictated my life, and setting boundaries or saying "No" seemed impossible.

For 21 years, I lived this way, feeling trapped and voiceless. But everything changed when I joined D Mantra, a life-transformative program led by Dr. Meghna Dikshit and Ms.Nayan Agarwal. Under their guidance, I had countless "bulb-on" moments that illuminated my life and reshaped my understanding of relationships—with others and myself.

I learned that setting boundaries is not selfish but necessary. Saying "No" to others when it means saying "Yes" to your happiness is an act of love, not defiance. I realized that constantly making yourself unhappy to please others only leads to resentment and exhaustion. True courage lies in meeting yourself, understanding your worth, and loving who you are.

This book reflects my journey and the wisdom I've gathered. It is for anyone who has ever felt trapped by societal conditioning, weighed down by expectations, or silenced by fear. Through examples of famous personalities who dared to challenge the norms—people like Oprah Winfrey, who overcame childhood adversity to become a global icon of resilience, or Malala Yousafzai, who fought for her education despite life-threatening opposition—you will see how courage can change lives in the most profound ways.

"Courage Can Change" will inspire you to take the first step toward your well-being, no matter how small. It will remind you that loving yourself is not selfish but essential. And most importantly, it will show you that with courage, you can rewrite your life story and live it on your terms.

Seeking help from others in your journey is also an act of courage. It takes bravery to admit that you cannot do it alone and to reach out for support when needed. Many people hesitate to ask for help, fearing judgment or appearing weak, but true strength lies in recognizing that we are not meant to navigate life's challenges entirely on our own.

If you can help yourself and find solutions independently, that's wonderful. However, if you struggle, don't hesitate to lean on others for guidance and support. Whether it's a mentor, a friend, a professional, or a loved one, their assistance can provide the clarity and strength you need to move forward.

Remember, taking help does not diminish your capabilities; instead, it equips you to rise above your challenges and grow stronger. The courage to seek help will pave the way for transformation and empower you to face life with newfound confidence and resilience.

Table Of Contents

Chapter #1

What Is Courage?

A journey of a thousand miles begins with a single step.

- Lao Tzu

When we think about courage, we often assume we fully understand it. We might believe there's no need to learn about it because we know what courage is and how it works. But when it's time to take action or apply courage in real life, many realize it's not as easy as we thought. The concept of courage can feel distant and hard to grasp when faced with a challenge.

In our daily lives, even in small situations, we often hesitate or take a step back instead of confronting challenges directly. We might evade tough issues or escape from challenging situations because we lack the courage to deal with them. But courage is essential to live fulfilling lives that reflect our desires and values.

Courage isn't just a topic to brush aside or something we don't need to learn about. It means knowing how to step forward, even when we're scared. When we know how to face our fears, we develop true courage. We see how much more beautiful and fulfilling life can become when we show courage in our everyday lives, even in small ways.

Courage shapes our lives, helping us overcome obstacles and pursue what matters to us. It's not just about big, heroic acts; it's about the little moments when we choose to move forward despite our fears. When we do this, life takes on a new and richer meaning, where we can achieve our goals and live authentically.

This concept varies between individuals and across different age groups. For a small child, courage might mean standing firm during a quarrel with a friend or simply taking an ant in their hand and touching it, conquering their fear of the tiny creature. For teenagers, courage can be seen in actions like breaking the rules or stepping outside the bounds of discipline, challenging the norms around them.

As people enter middle age, courage often takes the form of speaking up in front of authority figures, such as a boss or someone in a higher position, despite the potential consequences. For a soldier, courage means risking their life to protect others on the battlefield. For a teacher, it's the choice to work in challenging environments, like an inner-city school, to make a difference. A law enforcement officer shows courage by upholding integrity, even when tempted by a bribe. For a teenager, courage might be the strength to resist peer pressure and say no to drugs. For others, courage is the quiet resilience to endure hardship rather than betraying their beliefs or values. In relationships, courage is the strength to walk away from abuse and choose self-respect. Finally, someone might show courage by giving up a high-paying job to pursue a service life, prioritizing purpose over personal gain.

Throughout our lives, we've learned that showing our true selves and speaking without fear, especially in challenging situations, embodies the essence of courage. This understanding is often rooted in physical courage, the bravery to confront tangible fears and dangers.

Courage can also vary according to gender, as societal expectations and experiences often shape how individuals perceive and express courage. For women, courage usually involves challenging societal norms or expectations that have traditionally limited their roles. For instance, a woman might show courage by pursuing a career in a male-dominated field, challenging stereotypes, or speaking out against inequality and harassment. This form of courage often requires confronting deeply ingrained biases and overcoming the fear of being judged or marginalized.

On the other hand, for men, courage is sometimes associated with meeting expectations of strength, stoicism, or taking on risks that society traditionally associates with masculinity. For example, a man might demonstrate courage by showing vulnerability, asking for help, or expressing emotions openly, defying the stereotype that men must always be challenging and unemotional. Alternatively, he might show courage by protecting others in physically dangerous situations, fulfilling the traditional expectation of being a protector.

When we look in the dictionary and find words like bravery, daring, grit, boldness, or even punk, we look at more than just a list of definitions. Each word represents a distinct quality of courage or resilience that appeals to us differently. They all signify aspects of personal strength and the courage to stand out or push through adversity, yet each brings its unique flavor.

Take bravery, for example. It often invokes images of heroes who act selflessly in the face of danger. It's the courage to act even when fear is present. Daring is slightly different, carrying an element of risk-taking or willingness to venture into the unknown. It suggests a readiness to take a chance, perhaps without complete certainty of the outcome. Grit speaks to persistence, a tough resilience that keeps someone moving forward even through hardship and challenges, day after day. Boldness is the willingness to take risks, perhaps confidently or assertively, while punk often symbolizes defiance against norms—a rebellious spirit that refuses to conform to societal expectations.

These words resonate because they align with aspects of ourselves or the ideals we aspire to. They symbolize a powerful human instinct to seek strength, overcome limitations, and remain true to ourselves or our beliefs despite opposition. Each term reflects how people stand up, push forward, or stay unshaken. When we find words that embody these qualities, we hold tight to them as symbols of encouragement and empowerment, using them to inspire and define our paths. They remind us that courage is multifaceted and can be as simple as taking one more step forward or as daring as challenging the world around us.

These examples highlight that while courage is a universal concept, gender-specific experiences, and societal norms can influence its expression. Both forms of courage, whether challenging gender stereotypes or fulfilling them meaningfully, are vital and commendable in their own right.

Courage faces fear, pain, danger, uncertainty, or challenges despite feeling afraid or anxious. It involves making difficult decisions or taking actions that require inner strength and resolve, even when the outcome is uncertain. Courage can take many forms, such as standing up for what is right, speaking the truth, trying something new, or persevering through adversity. It's about doing what needs to be done, even when challenging or scary.

Courage can manifest in many ways, such as:

1. Physical courage: Showing bravery in physical danger or pain.

2. Moral courage: Standing up for what is right, even if it means going against the majority or facing criticism.

3. Emotional courage: Being vulnerable, sharing feelings, and facing emotional challenges head-on.

4. Intellectual courage: Embracing new ideas, questioning assumptions, and exploring unconventional perspectives.

5. Spiritual courage: Exploring and deepening one's beliefs, values, and connection to something greater.

However, all types of courage are essential in everyone's life. Whether facing a personal challenge, standing up for what is right, or dealing with unexpected dangers, courage is the key to overcoming obstacles and achieving success. For instance, students may need emotional courage to confront their fear of failure and persevere through difficult exams. Similarly, moral courage might be required to speak out against unfair workplace practices, even when it could lead to personal or professional repercussions. Physical courage becomes crucial when physical safety is at risk, such as when a firefighter runs into a burning building.

In every scenario, courage serves as a foundation for action. It empowers individuals to step out of their comfort zones, take risks, and face fears head-on. Without courage, we might avoid challenges or settle for less than we are capable of, but with it, we can push through difficulties, protect ourselves and others, and ultimately achieve our goals.

For example, consider someone who has always dreamed of starting a business. They might face numerous challenges, such as financial risks, fear of failure, and the uncertainty of leaving a stable job. Overcoming the fear of the unknown requires emotional courage, moral courage to stick to one's values and business ethics, and even physical courage to handle entrepreneurship's long hours and exhaustion. By embracing courage in all its forms, they can navigate these challenges and work towards building a successful business.

Thus, courage is not just a trait but a necessary tool for navigating life's complexities. It enables us to face problems and challenges with the confidence that, no matter the outcome, we have done our best to achieve success.

CHAPTER #2

COURAGE TO SAY "NO"

Whatever you do, you need courage. Whatever you decide, someone will always tell you you are wrong. Difficulties always tempt you to believe that your critics are right. To map out a course of action and follow it to an end requires some of the same courage that a soldier needs. Peace has its victories, but it takes brave men to win them.

- RALPH Waldo Emerson

Anjana was born and raised in Varanasi within a traditional North Indian joint family. From a young age, she faced numerous sacrifices, a reality shaped by her father's position as the younger brother. His elder brother controlled all family matters. Growing up, Anjana was constantly compelled to put aside her desires, even for the simplest things she needed.

In this strict household, where rules and regulations governed every aspect of life, Anjana learned early on that children were to remain silent and submissive in the presence of elders. She was taught to suppress her feelings and avoid expressing her needs or opinions. As a result, she struggled with a deep-seated sense of inadequacy, often feeling incapable and unworthy.

Over time, this environment eroded her confidence, leading her to believe she was inferior to others. She became a child who, though inherently kind and gentle, never spoke up or asserted herself, resigning to the belief that she was meant to remain in the background, unseen and unheard.

Anjana always dreamed of her married life as a chance to escape the constraints of her upbringing. She envisioned marrying a well-educated man and living in a beautiful home where she could finally be happy. In her mind, marriage was the key to a better future, a life where her dreams would come true.

However, after her marriage, Anjana's hopes were shattered. Her uncle arranged the marriage, leaving her parents powerless to intervene. It quickly became clear that the life she had imagined was not to be. Her dreams were broken, and she faced a reality far different from what she had longed for.

Anjana could not stand up for herself in her in-laws' family, as her nature had been shaped by years of submission and self-doubt. She lacked the courage to say no, even when faced with things she didn't like. She went through the motions, day and night, doing what was expected of her without question.

Despite managing her job, household responsibilities, and everything her in-laws required, Anjana couldn't muster the strength to assert her desires or opinions. She was trapped in a cycle of compliance and lacked the courage to change her circumstances.

Anjana lived much of her life without recognition or appreciation for her hard work and sacrifices. She felt invisible, with no one to understand her struggles. After 20 years of marriage, the loss of her mother plunged her into deep emotional trauma. She reached a point where she felt nothing left in the world for her, retreating into herself and shutting out everything around her.

But just when she thought all hope was lost, a mentor entered her life, bringing with them a light that began to dispel the darkness. With their guidance, Anjana started to groom herself, rediscovering the strength she had buried for so many years. She began to reflect on all that she had lost and all that she had endured.

For the first time, she realized the importance of valuing herself. Anjana understood that to make others happy, she first had to prioritize her happiness. This newfound perspective transformed her life, empowering her to stand tall and embrace the person she had always been meant to be.

Now, Anjana has found the courage she once lacked. She no longer hesitates to say no when something doesn't align with her desires or values. She has learned to prioritize herself, doing only what truly matters to her without taking on unnecessary burdens.

It took immense strength for Anjana to take that first step toward change, but it was a step that transformed her life. She now understands that reclaiming her voice and standing up for herself is not just an act of courage—it's a declaration of self-worth.

Courage is often seen as an extraordinary trait reserved for moments of great heroism or daring feats. However, Anjana's story reveals that courage usually lies in our quieter, everyday decisions to honor ourselves and our needs.

For years, Anjana lived in the shadows, unable to assert herself or challenge the expectations placed upon her. Her journey shows that courage isn't always about bold, immediate action; sometimes, it's about enduring in silence until the moment comes when we can no longer remain silent.

Taking that first step towards change—whether it's saying no for the first time, standing up for what you believe in, or simply choosing to put yourself first—requires immense inner strength. It means facing fears, overcoming doubts, and confronting the deep-seated beliefs that have kept us from realizing our true potential.

Courage is not the absence of fear but the decision to move forward despite it. For Anjana, finding the courage to say no was a declaration of self-respect, a moment where she chose to rewrite her narrative. Her story reminds us that courage begins with a single step, and though it may be small, its impact can be profound, rippling through every aspect of our lives.

In essence, courage bridges the life we've lived and the life we aspire to. It allows us to break free from the past, confront the present, and step into a future where we fully control our destiny.

The ability to say NO is one of the most extraordinary acts of courage and strength we can demonstrate. Often, we find it difficult to refuse our loved ones or those in positions of authority, whether it's a request for help, a task at work, or even a simple favor. Even when we don't have the time, energy, or desire to do something, we often agree, taking on additional burdens that cause us stress and discomfort.

This struggle usually stems from a desire to please others, avoid disappointing them, or keep them from feeling hurt or distant. We fear that saying no might damage our relationships, so we push ourselves beyond our limits, even when it means sacrificing our well-being.

However, saying no when necessary is crucial for living a balanced and fulfilling life. It's not just about refusing a request but valuing your time, energy, and needs. It's about understanding that you can't give your best to others if you constantly overextend yourself.

Consider the story of Joseph, a dedicated employee who always went the extra mile for his colleagues and bosses. He was known as the person who would never say NO, no matter how complex or time-consuming the task. His superiors often piled extra work on him because they knew he wouldn't refuse, and his friends frequently leaned on him for favors, knowing he would always agree.

Over time, Joseph found himself exhausted and overwhelmed, with little time for himself or his pursuits. He started feeling resentful but couldn't bring himself to say NO.

He feared people would think less of him and might be disappointed or even cut ties with him if he refused.

One day, after being asked to take on yet another project at work that he didn't have the capacity for, Joseph finally mustered the courage to say NO. He respectfully explained that he was at his limit and couldn't take on anything more without compromising the quality of his work. To his surprise, her boss appreciated his honesty and reassigned the project to someone else.

This small act of courage opened a new chapter in Joseph's life. He began setting boundaries, saying no when necessary, and prioritizing his well-being. As a result, he became more focused, productive, and much happier. His relationships didn't suffer as he had feared; they improved because he was no longer burdened by resentment.

Saying no is not about rejecting others but affirming your needs and limits. Prioritizing yourself takes immense courage, especially when you fear disappointing others. But by learning to say no, you protect your energy, maintain your well-being, and ultimately become more effective and present in all areas of your life. It's a small word with immense power, bringing balance and clarity to your life.

The two-letter word "NO" is simple, but saying it often requires great courage. Imagine, for instance, if specific individuals throughout history had not found the courage to say "NO" to injustice, oppression, or wrongdoing. The world as we know it might be very different today.

For example, Rosa Parks' refusal to give up her seat on a bus in Montgomery, Alabama, became a powerful symbol of resistance against racial segregation. Similarly, when leaders like Mahatma Gandhi and Martin Luther King Jr. said "NO" to violence and advocated for nonviolent resistance, they inspired movements that brought about significant social change.

Saying "no" can be difficult because it often means challenging the status quo, challenging others' expectations, or facing potential backlash. However, when used with conviction, this simple word can protect personal boundaries, uphold ethical principles, and even change the course of history.

The psychology behind saying "NO" is rooted in several social and personal factors. Here's an overview:

1. Fear of Rejection or Conflict

- Many people struggle with saying "NO" because they fear it will lead to rejection or conflict. They may worry that declining a request will make others angry, disappointed, or think less of them. This fear is often tied to a desire to maintain harmony in relationships and avoid uncomfortable confrontations.

2. Desire for Approval

- The need for social approval plays a significant role in people's reluctance to say NO. Many individuals are concerned with how others perceive them and want to be seen as kind, helpful, or agreeable. Saying "yes" feels like a way to gain or maintain approval from others.

3. Guilt and Obligation

- People often say yes out of guilt or a sense of obligation. They may feel responsible for helping others, especially in close relationships or communities, even if doing so costs them their well-being. This is common in people with a strong sense of duty or responsibility.

4. Fear of Missing Out (FOMO)

- Another psychological factor is the fear of missing out. Some individuals say "yes" because they worry that declining might cause them to miss out on opportunities, experiences, or social connections, leading to regret later.

5. People-Pleasing Personality

- Individuals with a people-pleasing personality often find it difficult to say NO. They derive self-worth from meeting others' expectations and making others happy, which makes saying no feel like a failure.

6. Low Self-Esteem

- People with low self-esteem may feel that their needs are not as important as others, making it harder to assert themselves. They might fear being seen as selfish or inconsiderate if they say NO, reinforcing the cycle of agreeing to things they don't want to do.

7. Conditioning and Social Norms

- Culturally, many are conditioned from a young age to be agreeable, obedient, and helpful. Saying "NO" is often associated with being rude or disrespectful, which can lead to internal resistance. Especially in some cultures, saying yes is seen as a sign of respect and politeness.

8. Cognitive Dissonance

- Cognitive dissonance occurs when there's a conflict between someone's values and their actions. If a person values their time but constantly says "yes," it can create internal discomfort. Yet, changing their behavior (saying "NO") requires confronting this discomfort, which is challenging.

9. Difficulty with Boundaries

- Setting boundaries requires self-awareness & assertiveness. Many people struggle to establish clear personal boundaries, fearing how others will react or feeling unsure about appropriate boundaries. Learning to say NO often involves building the skills to protect one's needs.

Overcoming the Difficulty of Saying "No"

- Awareness: Understanding the emotional & psychological reasons behind the reluctance to say no.

- Practice: Gradually practicing assertiveness & boundary-setting.

- Self-Worth: Reinforcing self-esteem and realizing that it's okay to prioritize one's own needs.

- Reframing: Viewing "NO" as a healthy response that respects personal limits rather than as something negative or selfish.

Being able to say "NO" is an essential part of self-care and maintaining mental health, especially in managing relationships and personal boundaries.

Courage is pivotal in overcoming the difficulty of saying "NO" because it involves facing fears, discomfort, and potential social repercussions. Here's how courage can help:

1. Facing Fear of Rejection

- Courage helps confront the fear of rejection. It allows a person to acknowledge that saying "NO" might lead to disappointment or rejection from others, but it's necessary for self-care and well-being. Instead of avoiding the risk, courageous individuals face it head-on, accepting that they cannot always please everyone.

2. Overcoming Fear of Conflict

- Many people say "yes" to avoid conflict. Courage allows you to embrace the possibility of disagreement or confrontation and trust that the relationship can withstand it. Individuals can assert their needs without feeling overly anxious about potential backlash by being courageous.

3. Breaking the People-Pleasing Habit

- It takes bravery to challenge ingrained habits like people-pleasing. Courage allows people to question the automatic response of always saying yes, realizing it's okay to disappoint others sometimes. Defying internal programming requires courage because it disrupts comfort zones and longstanding behavior patterns.

4. Building Self-Esteem

- Low self-esteem often leads to saying yes because others' needs are more important than one's own. Courage is the bridge to building self-esteem because each act of saying no reinforces a sense of self-worth. Over time, courage leads to the realization that one's feelings, time, and boundaries are equally important.

5. Standing Up for Your Boundaries

- Courage allows you to stand firm in your boundaries, even when others challenge you. It takes bravery to declare what is acceptable or not in a relationship or interaction and even more so to enforce those boundaries. Courage helps individuals resist pressure, guilt, or manipulation from others, especially in complex relationships.

6. Resisting Social Conditioning

- Social norms and conditioning often tell us to be agreeable, especially in certain cultures or family dynamics. Courage enables people to push back against societal expectations and assert their individuality. It takes boldness to challenge what we've been taught from a young age about always being accommodating or obedient.

7. Dealing with Cognitive Dissonance

- When someone says "yes" against their genuine desire, they experience cognitive dissonance—a conflict between their actions and values. Courage helps people live in alignment with their values by empowering them to say "no" when necessary. This reduces inner conflict and promotes personal integrity.

8. Taking Responsibility for One's Well-being

- Courage means prioritizing mental, emotional, and physical health, even when difficult. It's about taking responsibility for your needs and understanding that self-care is not selfish but essential. Saying no becomes an act of bravery that fosters long-term well-being.

9. Developing Assertiveness

- Assertiveness requires courage. Many fear being assertive will make them seem rude, demanding, or selfish. Courage helps people realize that assertiveness is a balanced and healthy way to communicate—direct but not aggressive. It allows people to express their needs with confidence and clarity.

10. Pushing Through Discomfort

- The process of learning to say "NO" can be uncomfortable and anxiety-provoking at first. Courage enables people to push through this discomfort, knowing that it will lead to personal growth and healthier relationships in the long term. Over time, courage transforms the initial unease into a sense of empowerment.

Courage is the key that unlocks the ability to say "NO" without fear, guilt, or anxiety. It empowers individuals to prioritize their needs, establish healthy boundaries, and live in alignment with their values, leading to healthier relationships and greater self-respect.

Historically, moments of transformation have often begun with simply saying "NO" to injustice or oppressive norms. Consider Mahatma Gandhi and the Salt March of 1930. If Gandhi had accepted the British-imposed Salt Act, which taxed necessities of life, India's fight for independence might have followed a different course. By refusing to comply, Gandhi highlighted how unjust and exploitative colonial rule was, turning an everyday commodity into a symbol of resistance. His defiance inspired millions, demonstrating how a single refusal to accept injustice can shake the foundations of power.

Similarly, Rosa Parks' courageous refusal to give up her bus seat in 1955 sparked the Montgomery Bus Boycott, a pivotal moment in the Civil Rights Movement in the United States. Her act of defiance was not just about a seat on a bus; it was a rejection of the systemic racism that permeated American society. Had she not said "NO" that day, the movement for racial equality might not have gained the momentum it did at that crucial moment. Parks' stand against discrimination became a powerful symbol of how one person's refusal to accept oppression can ignite widespread change.

Throughout history, we see countless examples of individuals who dared to say "NO" when it mattered most. This courage—the courage to stand up against what is wrong—often sets the wheels of progress in motion. Whether in historical events or mythology, where many heroes and heroines defied norms and resisted oppression, the power of "NO" is undeniable. Saying "NO" is not just an act of resistance but an assertion of dignity, self-worth, and justice.

This courage is also seen in personal lives and individual stories. For instance, the story of Anjana, who found the strength to say "NO" to the life imposed on her, teaches us the profound value of standing up for oneself.

Her decision to break free from the emotional trauma and find her path is an inspiring reminder that the courage to say "NO" is often the first step toward reclaiming one's life and happiness.

In all these examples—Gandhi, Parks, Anjana—we see that saying "NO" requires immense courage, but it is also the key to unlocking change. Whether on a societal or personal level, the ability to stand up against injustice and refuse what does not serve you or society is essential to achieving success and creating a better world. It teaches us that even the seemingly impossible can become achievable with courage.

The word "NO," though simple and short, holds significant power in shaping our lives and boundaries. Saying "NO" is an act of courage because it allows us to protect our time, energy, and values.

It helps us avoid overcommitting, maintain self-respect, and prioritize what truly matters. Saying "NO" to things that don't align with our goals or well-being is essential for personal growth, mental peace, and healthy relationships. While it can sometimes feel uncomfortable, it's necessary for asserting one's limits and creating a balanced, fulfilling life.

CHAPTER #3

COURAGEOUS LEADERSHIP

One aspect of leadership that isn't talked about enough is courage. To lead with courage is not merely to take bold steps but to do so with an unflinching resolve, a sound ethical compass, and a vision of success that beckons even the most reluctant followers.

But what does it mean to be a courageous leader, and how can one cultivate this virtue to foster personal and professional growth?

Nelson Mandela's life is a profound testament to the power of courage in the face of adversity. Born in 1918 in South Africa, Mandela grew up under the harsh realities of apartheid, a system that institutionalized racial segregation and discrimination. From an early age, he witnessed the injustice and inequality that plagued his country, fueling his desire to fight for freedom and equality for all South Africans.

Mandela's journey of courage began when he joined the African National Congress (ANC) in 1943, actively participating in its struggle against apartheid. Over the years, he became a key figure in the movement, advocating for nonviolent resistance. However, when the South African government brutally suppressed peaceful protests, Mandela and others realized that more aggressive measures were necessary. He co-founded the ANC's armed wing, Umkhonto we Sizwe, and embraced armed struggle as a last resort to fight the oppressive regime.

Mandela's courage was tested when he was arrested in 1962 and sentenced to life imprisonment in 1964. For 27 long years, he endured the hardships of prison life, much of it spent in the infamous Robben Island prison. Despite the physical and emotional toll of imprisonment, Mandela never wavered in his belief that South Africa would one day be free. His courage was in his resistance to oppression and his ability to maintain hope, dignity, and resolve in despair.

During his time in prison, Mandela became a symbol of the anti-apartheid struggle in South Africa and worldwide. His courage inspired countless individuals to continue the fight for freedom. In the late 1980s, as international pressure on South Africa grew and internal unrest escalated, the apartheid government began negotiations for Mandela's release. In 1990, after nearly three decades behind bars, Mandela walked free, greeted as a hero by millions.

However, Mandela's greatest act of courage came after his release. Rather than seeking revenge or fueling division, he advocated for reconciliation between South Africa's racial groups. He understood that true freedom would only come through unity, forgiveness, and a commitment to building a democratic nation. In 1994, Mandela was elected South Africa's first Black president in the country's first multiracial elections.

Throughout his life, Nelson Mandela's courage was about standing up against oppression and choosing the path of peace and reconciliation, even when it would have been easier to harbor resentment. His bravery transformed a divided nation and left an enduring legacy of justice, equality, and the power of forgiveness. His life reminds us that courage is not just about confronting external enemies but also about overcoming internal struggles and making choices that uplift humanity.

Being courageous means navigating through uncertainty with confidence and making decisions that might not be popular but are necessary. It involves standing up for what is right, even when challenging, and encouraging others to voice their ideas and concerns. These types of leader advocate for change, are transparent about the challenges ahead, and inspire their teams to strive for excellence despite the odds.

Essence of Courageous Leadership

Courage in leadership transcends the realm of bold, impulsive action; at its core, it's a strategic undertaking. Authentic, courageous leadership manifests in several key behaviors:

- Vulnerability: A courageous leader is not afraid to show their humanity, admitting to their limitations and being open to learning from those around them.

- Transparency: Communicating openly, even when confronting brutal truths, is a hallmark of successful leaders.

- Empowerment: Courageous leaders inspire individuals within their teams to act boldly, creating a culture that applauds initiative.

Building A Courage Leadership Strategy

Once you've ascended to a leadership role, the quest for courage does not end; it simply takes on a new dimension. It's about establishing your presence and fostering a culture that embraces innovation and decisive action.

Cultivate A Growth Mindset

Solidifying a growth mindset is fundamental as it steers your focus from what you can't do to what you can learn. It's about viewing challenges as opportunities for a personal mindset shift that equips you to adapt and persevere in adversity and uncertainty.

Strategies:

- Challenge negative self-talk and fixed beliefs about your abilities.

- Mindfully engage with setbacks, identifying lessons for future resilience.

- Celebrate incremental successes and reflect on the progress made.

Leverage Emotional Intelligence

Leading a team, you'll inevitably encounter moments of doubt, anxiety, and fear. Understanding and managing your emotions is an asset. Emotional intelligence enables precise decision-making, effective communication, and robust stress management.

Approaches:

- Enhance self-awareness through regular reflection and feedback.

- Practice empathy in professional interactions to build rapport and trust.

- Engage in stress-reducing activities such as meditation or exercise.

Calculated Risks

Becoming a courageous leader is a conscious and iterative process. It begins with self-awareness and extends to the perpetual pursuit of wisdom and insight. A significant step is experimenting with risk; it's about making calculated decisions that push you and your team beyond your comfort zone but within sensible risks that align with your vision and mission.

Making calculated risks involve:

- Evaluate the Potential Outcomes: Before taking a risk, thoroughly analyze the potential positive and negative outcomes. Consider the best and worst-case scenarios to prepare for any possibility.

- Gather and Analyse Data: Collect relevant data and insights to make informed decisions. Use this information to assess the feasibility and potential impact of the risk.

- Set Clear Objectives: Define what you aim to achieve by taking this risk. Having clear goals helps assess the risk's worthiness and aligns your actions with your long-term vision.

- Implement Risk Mitigation Strategies: Identify ways to minimize potential downsides. This could involve phased approaches, contingency planning, or setting aside resources to handle unexpected outcomes.

- Monitor and Adjust: After taking a risk, closely monitor the outcomes and be prepared to make adjustments as necessary. Adaptability and responsiveness to developments can help mitigate losses and capitalize on emerging opportunities.

Continuing to Lead

Maintaining courage in leadership, especially after holding a position for an extended period, ensures ongoing innovation and adaptability. It sends a powerful message of resilience and commitment to progress, inspiring the team to pursue excellence regardless of tenure.

For leaders already in position, steps to deepen your courage include:

- Step Up to Decision-Making: Don't shy away from tough choices. Analyse data, seek advice, but ultimately, make a call and stand by it.

- Model Courageous Behavior: Your team will look to you for cues on how to act. Demonstrate your courage in actions and words, earning their respect and encouraging their bravery.

- Coach and Mentor: The willingness to develop others is part of courageous leadership. Invest time in coaching and mentorship, guiding the next generation of leaders to greater heights.

By consistently displaying courage in your leadership, you enhance your capabilities and set a ripple effect that empowers others to follow suit. The road to courageous leadership promises success and a legacy of inspiration and transformation.

Courageous leadership isn't just about standing firm in the face of adversity; it's about inspiring others to do the same. By embracing self-awareness, vision, resilience, and integrity, leaders can build teams and organizations equipped to face challenges, innovate, and thrive in an ever-changing world. Courage in leadership creates an immediate impact and a lasting legacy, showing that authentic leadership comes from making bold, ethical decisions that elevate individuals and society.

In the heart of the Swat Valley in Pakistan, a young girl named Malala Yousafzai emerged as a beacon of hope and courage in a world fraught with danger and oppression. Malala was raised in a region where the Taliban's influence loomed large, and girls were often denied the right to education. She was passionate about learning from a young age and firmly believed every girl deserved an education.

Malala's father, Ziauddin Yousafzai, was an educator and an outspoken advocate for girls' education. He instilled in her the values of empowerment and resilience. Inspired by her father, Malala began speaking out against the injustices faced by girls in her community. At just 11 years old, she started writing a blog for the BBC Urdu under a pseudonym, sharing her experiences and the struggles of girls seeking education amidst the chaos of conflict.

Her voice resonated far beyond the borders of her valley. She became a symbol of hope, courage, and determination, advocating for the right to education even as the threats against her grew. Malala's bravery did not go unnoticed and quickly garnered international attention. However, this newfound fame also made her a target.

One day, as she was returning home from school, Malala was shot in the head by a Taliban gunman. The attack was a horrific attempt to silence her voice, but it only amplified her message. Miraculously, Malala survived the assassination attempt and was flown to the UK for treatment. Her recovery was not just physical; it began an even more remarkable journey.

Instead of retreating in fear, Malala emerged more assertive and determined than ever. She began speaking out on global platforms, advocating for girls' education and the importance of fighting against oppression. Her courage inspired millions worldwide, and she became a symbol of resilience and strength.

Malala was awarded the Nobel Peace Prize at 17, making her the youngest laureate in history. During her acceptance speech, she passionately advocated the power of education and the need for every child to have the opportunity to learn. She emphasized that education is a fundamental human right and that no one should be denied this right, regardless of gender or circumstances.

Malala's story is one of extraordinary bravery and unwavering commitment to justice. She has traveled the world, meeting with world leaders, advocating for education, and continuing her fight against oppression. Through the Malala Fund, she ensures that girls everywhere have access to education and the chance to achieve their dreams.

Today, Malala Yousafzai is a testament to one voice's power to change the world. Her courage in adversity inspires countless individuals to stand up for their rights and fight for a better future. In a world where girls' education is still under threat, Malala's journey reminds us that bravery can ignite change and that pursuing knowledge can transform lives and societies.

People who confront challenges with courage and bravery often emerge as inspiring figures capable of overcoming seemingly insurmountable obstacles. Their strength in facing adversity serves as a beacon of hope for others, encouraging those around them to pursue their paths with determination and resilience.

These courageous individuals become symbols of inspiration and motivation, showing that it is possible to rise above difficulties and fight against what is unjust or harmful to society. Their stories resonate deeply with others, igniting a spark of courage within those who may feel trapped by their circumstances. By sharing their experiences and demonstrating unwavering resolve, they empower others to stand up for themselves and their beliefs.

As people witness the remarkable journeys of these brave individuals, they are often motivated to follow in their footsteps. This collective inspiration can create a ripple effect, encouraging more people to confront their fears and challenges head-on. Ultimately, this courage can lead to personal growth, enabling individuals to reach their goals and fulfill their desires.

In this way, the courage of a few can uplift the many, fostering a culture of resilience and empowerment. By embracing bravery in the face of adversity, individuals can transform their struggles into stepping stones toward achieving their dreams and making a meaningful impact on their own lives and the lives of others.

CHAPTER #4

COURAGE TO FACE FEAR

Courage is not the absence of fear, but rather the judgment that something else is more important than fear.

- Ambrose Redmoon

When Pan Am Flight 73, Pen route from Mumbai to New York, was hijacked by terrorists belonging to the Abu Nidal Organization after a stopover in Karachi, Pakistan. The 17-hour ordeal that followed was a crucible of fear.

Passengers and crew were boarding and settling in for the flight from Karachi to Frankfurt, with a stopover planned in Frankfurt before heading to New York. The atmosphere was typical for an international flight, with people chatting, reading, or resting. Suddenly, heavily armed terrorists in uniforms forced their way onto the plane, creating immediate confusion and fear. The situation quickly escalated as the hijackers, who were members of the Abu Nidal Organization, seized control of the aircraft.

The hijackers, who were armed with guns and grenades, ordered everyone to remain seated and threatened violence if anyone disobeyed. Communication between the cockpit and the cabin broke down as the pilots managed to escape through a cockpit window, leaving the flight crew in the passenger cabin to face the hijackers. Passengers would have started whispering anxiously, some trying to comfort each other while others remained frozen with fear.

The cabin crew, led by senior flight attendant Neerja Bhanot, tried to keep passengers calm and safe. Bhanot and her team were instrumental in hiding the passports of American citizens, as the hijackers were mainly targeting U.S. passengers. The crew's discreet acts of heroism aimed to protect the passengers from further danger.

As time passed, the hijackers made demands to release prisoners and fueled tensions with threats and displays of their weapons. The passengers were ordered to keep their heads down and remain silent. Negotiations with the authorities outside the plane dragged on, heightening the anxiety within the cabin. Conditions inside the plane became increasingly tense, with limited food, water, and toilet access, leading to physical and emotional strain among the passengers.

The passengers, a mix of men, women, and children from different nationalities, were trapped in an agonizing wait as the hours turned into a full day. Some people might have prayed silently, while others tried to maintain composure or comfort their loved ones. The oppressive heat in the cabin, combined with the psychological pressure of the hijackers' threats, added to the suffocating atmosphere.

After approximately 16 hours of the standoff, tensions reached a breaking point when power to the aircraft failed. In the darkness and confusion, the hijackers opened fire and threw grenades at the passengers. The cabin erupted in panic and chaos as passengers scrambled to escape, some using emergency exits and slides. The brave actions of crew members like Neerja Bhanot helped many passengers escape, but significant casualties remained.

It is natural to imagine that Neerja felt intense fear when the four heavily armed hijackers stormed the plane, shouting threats and brandishing guns and grenades. The fear of violence, injury, or death would have been overwhelming, especially considering the uncertainty of the hijackers' intentions. Neerja would have been acutely aware of the potential for harm not just to herself but to her fellow crew members and passengers, heightening her sense of responsibility and anxiety. Witnessing terrified passengers and seeing the grim determination on the faces of the hijackers likely deepened her fears.

Despite this fear, Neerja displayed remarkable courage throughout the ordeal. Her initial reaction was not one of paralysis but of resolve. She immediately took steps to alert the pilots, allowing them to escape through the cockpit window and deny the hijackers complete control of the plane. With the pilots gone, Neerja understood that the safety of everyone on board now rested mainly on her actions.

Her courage was most evident in her priority of protecting the passengers. She demonstrated quick thinking by hiding American passports, knowing that U.S. citizens were the hijackers' primary targets. This act alone saved many lives and showed how she overcame her fear to think strategically for the greater good. Throughout the 16-hour ordeal, she worked to maintain calm among passengers, offering reassurance and silently coordinating with her crew to ensure as much safety as possible.

The most poignant display of Neerja's bravery came during the chaotic moments when the hijackers began firing indiscriminately after the power failure. In the face of direct violence and imminent danger, Neerja opened an emergency exit and guided passengers to safety. She could have been among the first to flee the aircraft, but she chose to help others escape, ensuring that children and those nearest to her were safe. In her final act of courage, she shielded three children from gunfire, ultimately sacrificing her own life to protect them.

Her courage went beyond the absence of fear; it was about overcoming that fear to do what was necessary and proper in a crisis. Her bravery came from a profound sense of duty, empathy, and the unwavering belief that it was her responsibility to safeguard others. Even when confronted with death, Neerja's focus remained on saving lives. This blend of fear and courage made her an enduring symbol of heroism, recognized posthumously with awards such as the Ashok Chakra, India's highest peacetime gallantry award.

Although Neerja Bhanot's fear was undoubtedly genuine, her courage was stronger. It propelled her to act selflessly in the face of overwhelming danger, leaving an inspirational legacy of heroism and compassion.

Fear is the most formidable opponent we will ever face. When we allow fear to dominate our thoughts and actions, we are defeated before we begin. True courage is acknowledging fear but choosing to move forward regardless, knowing that the most significant battle is within our minds.

Fear is a natural emotion, a part of our human experience at various points in our lives. It's okay to feel fear—a response that can protect us and make us aware of our challenges. However, the key lies not in avoiding fear but in how we choose to respond to it.

Courage isn't the absence of fear; it's the strength to confront and overcome it. When we muster the courage to face our fears head-on, we unlock the potential for growth and transformation. Stepping out of the shadows of fear is a pivotal moment—we begin to see the world in a new light, where opportunities and possibilities start to unfold.

This process of moving beyond fear is essential. It's a journey leading us to a place of renewed understanding and insight into our lives. By confronting what scares us, we break free from the chains that hold us back, allowing us to move forward with greater confidence and clarity.

We discover a new sense of purpose and direction as we emerge from fear. Overcoming fear doesn't just bring relief; it brings empowerment. We realize that we can achieve far more than we once believed possible. We move closer to our goals with each step beyond our fears, and the path ahead becomes more apparent.

In essence, fear is not a barrier but a stepping stone. When faced with courage, it's a challenge that leads to personal growth and realizing our true potential. By embracing and overcoming our fears, we open the door to a brighter, more fulfilling future where we can achieve anything we set our minds to.

Navigating fear can be challenging, but there are several helpful steps you can take to manage and overcome it. Here's a structured approach to dealing with fear effectively:

1. Acknowledge Your Fear

- Identify the Fear: Take a moment to pinpoint your fear. Is it fear of failure, rejection, or the unknown? Understanding the specific fear is the first step in addressing it.

- Accept Your Feelings: Recognize that it's normal to feel fear. Accepting your emotions can help reduce their intensity and make them easier to manage.

2. Annalise the Fear

- Evaluate the Source: Consider what triggers your fear. Is it based on experience, societal pressure, or personal insecurities?

- Challenge Negative Thoughts: Reflect on the thoughts associated with your fear. Are they rational? Challenge any irrational beliefs or assumptions that may be fueling your fear.

3. Educate Yourself

- Gather Information: Often, fear is rooted in the unknown. Researching and learning about what you fear can help demystify it and reduce anxiety.

- Seek Advice: Talk to others who have faced similar fears or consult a professional. Hearing their experiences can provide perspective and strategies.

4. Develop a Plan

- Set Small Goals: Break down your fear into manageable steps. Set achievable goals that gradually lead you to confront and overcome your fear.

- Create an Action Plan: Outline the steps you will take to address your fear. A clear plan can provide structure and increase your confidence.

5. Practice Mindfulness and Relaxation Techniques

- Deep Breathing: Engage in deep breathing exercises to calm your mind and body. Focus on your breath to help ground yourself in the present moment.

- Meditation & Visualization: Use meditation or visualization techniques to imagine successfully facing your fear. This can help build confidence and reduce anxiety.

6. Take Action

- Face Your Fear Gradually: Start taking small steps toward confronting your fear. Gradually expose yourself to the situation that causes anxiety, starting with less intimidating aspects.

- Embrace Discomfort: Understand that discomfort is part of the process. Embracing it can help you build resilience and confidence.

7. Reflect and Adjust

- Evaluate Your Progress: After taking action, reflect on your experiences. What worked? What didn't? Use this feedback to adjust your approach.

- Celebrate Small Wins: Acknowledge and celebrate your progress, no matter how small. This can boost your motivation and reinforce positive behavior.

8. Seek Support

- Talk to Someone: Share your fears with friends, family, or a therapist. Their support can encourage and help you feel less isolated.

- Join Support Groups: Consider joining groups or communities where others share similar fears. Connecting with others can provide motivation and new insights.

9. Build Resilience

- Practice Self-Compassion: Be kind to yourself during this journey. Understand that everyone experiences fear, and it's okay to struggle.

- Develop a Growth Mindset: View challenges as opportunities for growth. Adopting a mindset that embraces learning can help you face fears more effectively.

10. Stay Committed

- Persevere: Overcoming fear is often a gradual process. Stay committed to your goals, and remember that setbacks are a natural part of growth.

- Reassess and Iterate: Periodically reassess your fears and progress. Adjust your strategies as needed to continue moving forward.

By following these steps, you can develop a practical approach to navigating fear, transforming it from a barrier into a catalyst for growth and resilience.

Swami Vivekananda, a saint, philosopher, and motivational speaker, is remembered as a beacon of inspiration, especially for the youth. He played a significant role in representing India on the world stage and is revered for his spiritual teachings and profound insights.

One notable story from his childhood highlights the seeds of greatness planted early in his life. Swami Vivekananda, then known as Narendranath Datta, displayed remarkable courage, intelligence, and an insatiable curiosity about life and spirituality as a young boy.

Once, while playing with his friends, Narendranath climbed a tree in his neighborhood, which the tree owner forbade the children from doing. To scare the boys, the owner told them that a demon was living in the tree and anyone who climbed it would be caught and harmed. While the other boys got scared and immediately climbed down, young Narendranath refused to be frightened. With confidence, he said, "If there were a demon, it would have caught me by now!"

This story reflects his fearlessness and strong belief in rational thinking. Even as a child, Swami Vivekananda questioned unquestioning beliefs and superstitions, displaying the qualities that would later make him a revered spiritual leader. His boldness, confidence, and critical thinking became defining traits throughout his life, influencing how he inspired countless people.

We can use logic to overcome fear. Why do we fail to become courageous, or why do we remain timid? The main reason is fear itself. But interestingly, it is this very fear that can make us brave. Being courageous doesn't mean you don't feel fear, avoid risk, or never face danger. Instead, courage is about overcoming fear, facing challenges head-on, and coming out stronger on the other side. Even the most courageous people experience fear, but what sets them apart is their ability to push past it and take action despite it. Whenever you feel afraid, examine your fear in detail. When analyzed with wisdom, many worries are not that frightening. Unknown fears, about which you are unaware, can scare you for no reason.

The solution is to get to the root of it and eliminate it. Some of these fears may be genuine, but the rest might be baseless. Due to a lack of clarity, our fear overwhelms us. When you clearly understand something and confine it within a boundary, you also grasp its outline, which helps you estimate its significance. But when something is unclear, and you have no knowledge about it, you cannot determine any threat's size.

In this state, your mind overestimates the danger or fear. However, the solution is not to stop thinking about your fear altogether. The more you think about it, the better you will be able to gauge its potential and scope. This means you shouldn't turn away from the things that scare you. Because doing so will make those things seem even more dangerous. Look into the eyes of your fear so that you can gauge its size.

The concept of fear setting was introduced by Tim Ferriss, an entrepreneur, public speaker, and best-selling author of The 4-Hour Workweek. This powerful tool emerged to help individuals navigate uncertainty, make informed decisions, and overcome the paralysis that often accompanies fear. (Fear setting list is given at the end)

At its core, fear setting is a structured exercise designed to help individuals clearly define their fears, assess potential worst-case scenarios, and prepare action plans to mitigate them. Unlike traditional goal setting, which emphasizes aspirations and desired outcomes, fear setting confronts the negative "what-ifs" that can obstruct progress.

To fully understand and benefit from Fear Setting, you first must understand Stoicism. Stoicism is "the endurance of pain or hardship without a display of feelings and complaint." Athletes and coaches are great examples of stoic individuals because they constantly face difficult decisions on TV and in the spotlight.

Take Tom Brady, quarterback for the world-champion New England Patriots. When he steps back to pass, 300-pound athletes charge in every direction, solely focused on crushing Brady before he throws the ball.

Whether Brady is crushed, throws an interception, or an incomplete pass, he remains stoic. He practices staying mentally tough without emotion or complaint so he's better mentally prepared for the next play.

Ferriss developed a "Fear Setting " tool to guide the path to stoicism. Fear Setting is a three-page checklist of one's fears and the possible results of action or inaction.

Fear Setting is "An operating system for thriving in high-stress environments. It's a way to visualize all the bad things that could happen to you so you become less afraid of taking action.

Now, imagine doing and saying the things we avoid for a brief moment.

Are you afraid of quitting your stressful job?
Are you afraid to speak your mind to a friend or spouse?
Are you afraid to ask for a raise you deserve?
Are you afraid to take a year off your life?
Are you afraid to ask for forgiveness?

Often, these are the exact things we need to do to be more successful, which is why Fear Setting is important.

Fear only holds power over us if we allow it to dominate our thoughts and actions. It thrives in the shadows of avoidance and hesitation, growing larger as we avoid confronting it. Fear, whether it's the fear of failure, rejection, the unknown, or any other challenge, gains strength from our reluctance to face it.

However, its grip loosens when we muster the courage to face our fear. When we confront it head-on, we realize that the magnitude of our fear is often an illusion, amplified by our minds. By showing bravery, no matter how daunting the situation may seem, fear starts to shrink, revealing itself to be much smaller and more manageable than we initially thought.

In essence, fear is only as powerful as we make it. Once we confront it with determination and courage, we strip it of its control over us. What once seemed insurmountable gradually diminishes in size, allowing us to grow stronger and more confident with every step we take. This transformation empowers us to overcome specific fears and instills a deep sense of resilience, enabling us to face future challenges with greater confidence and strength.

CHAPTER 5

THE NATURE AND SCIENCE OF COURAGE

Courage is the mental or moral strength to venture into, persevere through, and withstand danger, fear, or difficulty. It has been an essential trait in human evolution and survival.

From a psychological and biological perspective, courage is often seen as the ability to confront fears and take action despite feeling anxious or uncertain.

We tend to be over-confident about our courage. A study by Carnegie Mellon University found that people tend to overestimate the extent to which they will take action—for themselves or others—when faced with a dangerous situation. Thus, courage is built over time through repetition and experience more than through imagination.

Key regions of the brain also drive courage. A Weizmann Institute of Science study in Rehovot found that when people display courage, their frontal and temporal brain regions are most involved.

These are the areas responsible for decision-making for perception and memory. In moments of courage, we collect information, assess, determine the best reactions, and then cement the experience into memory for the next moment when courage is necessary.

The Nature of Courage

1. Moral and Physical Courage:

Moral Courage involves standing up for what is right, even when facing opposition or potential personal loss. It requires ethical awareness and a strong sense of integrity.

Physical Courage involves overcoming the fear of bodily harm, whether in life-threatening situations or challenges requiring endurance and strength.

2. Courage and Fear:

Courage is not the absence of fear but the ability to act in the face of it. Fear is a natural response to perceived threats, but courage enables individuals to push beyond their fears and still take action.

3. Emotional Courage:

Emotional courage involves embracing vulnerability, expressing emotions, and confronting internal struggles such as trauma, grief, or change. It is vital for personal growth and deep connections with others.

The Science of Courage

1. Neuroscience of Courage:

Amygdala: The amygdala plays a key role in the response to fear. Courage can be seen as the ability to regulate and manage the amygdala's fear-inducing signals.

Prefrontal Cortex: The prefrontal cortex, responsible for reasoning and decision-making, helps suppress the fear responses triggered by the amygdala. It allows individuals to assess risks and act rationally in high-stress situations.

2. Hormonal Influence:

Adrenaline: When courage is required, the body releases adrenaline, which boosts physical readiness, increases focus, and enhances decision-making speed. However, this "fight or flight" hormone can also escalate fear, making courage an act of balancing its effects.

Oxytocin is a hormone associated with social bonding and can promote courage in social situations. It helps individuals step up in the presence of loved ones or act altruistically in group contexts.

3. Resilience and Courage:

Studies show resilience—the ability to bounce back from adversity—strengthens courage. People with a resilient mindset are better equipped to take courageous actions because they trust their ability to recover from failure.

Building Courage

1. Mindfulness and Emotional Regulation:

Practices like mindfulness and meditation help individuals manage fear by enhancing awareness of their emotions. Emotional regulation techniques can strengthen the prefrontal cortex, allowing for better control over fear responses.

2. Incremental Exposure:

Gradual exposure to feared situations builds courage over time. Psychologically, this method allows the brain to desensitize fear triggers, making courageous behavior more attainable.

3. Support Systems:

Social support plays a critical role in fostering courage. Knowing that others believe in your ability to overcome obstacles can boost confidence, leading to more courageous actions.

Courage is a complex and multifaceted trait deeply rooted in human psychology, biology, and social context. By understanding its nature and science, individuals can cultivate the courage to confront fears, take risks, and grow in moral and emotional strength.

Types of Courage

You can demonstrate courage in various ways; not all are defined by self-motivated action. Courage involves choices that affect others and cause you to move forward or hold back—based on your discretion.

Stand With. Sometimes, a colleague may need support, and you can express your bravery by standing with them. If a co-worker has been wronged, overlooked, or verbally dismissed, it is a great time to stand with them. When a boss belittles a co-worker in a meeting, you can speak up, reinforcing her performance. You can stand with teammates constructively, firmly, and determinedly.

Stand Up. You can also demonstrate bravery by being yourself and owning your performance. Be assertive in expressing your talents, but also be open in expressing where you don't know it all. Own your mistakes and seek feedback about how to be better. Keep commitments, follow through, and avoid stalling or procrastinating. Take responsibility when you perform brilliantly, but also when you misstep and know you can do better. Accountability requires courage because when you do well, you must be confident enough to feel good about your success, and when you can do better, you must be confident enough to admit the gap and fill it. Being courageous about your performance allows you to grow.

Stand For. Express your courage through your values as well. Do the right thing for yourself, but also for others, as a member of a community. A study by Ohio State University found that students rated higher on courage, empathy, and honesty when they didn't cheat. And they also tended to believe more in the honesty of others around them. Their courage had important components that connected them to others (empathy and belief in the positive nature of others) and which contributed to their integrity (honesty). Know what matters most to you, and don't be shy about articulating your views. Do this so others can hear you and seek to learn from you. Open yourself to others to gain new perspectives and develop your opinions. As the saying goes, "When you know better, do better." Start with a firmly held belief and seek to expand your understanding of different perspectives to ensure your responses are as empathetic and holistic as possible.

Stand Down. Sometimes, the most courageous action is to step away or to compromise. True courage includes discerning what matters most and where you'll expend energy. It is choosing your battles and letting go when they are not as critical. Real courage isn't truculent or reckless—fighting at every turn. It is the ability to pause, consider, and act with discretion. Compromising can be the best of courage. You represent your values or those of your group, listen to others' preferences, and then find creative ways to meet the needs of the whole as much as possible—and keep things moving ahead.

Still Standing. Courage is also demonstrated over time when you persevere. You may be turned down for the promotion on your first try, and being brave means putting yourself out there again (and again). You may go through multiple rounds of interviews, but grit requires you to keep at it and maintain your confidence and grace. You also demonstrate courage through creativity. If you don't succeed at first, you may need to find a novel way to solve the problem or an innovative solution that surprises the system. A hallmark of courage is to keep at it, even when the process is complicated.

How to Demonstrate Courage

To demonstrate courage, you need just a few points of knowledge.

First, know yourself. Understand your goals and values to decide which actions matter most. Specific career goals may motivate you to take that expat role or reach for the next job that will stretch your skills. Your values will dictate which issues require your actions. Also, know your emotional responses. If you're going over the cliff of anger, it may be best to pause and consider your best action.

Also, know your limits. Often, growth requires you to leave your comfort zone and embrace new situations, take new actions, or venture out despite being unsure or afraid. Introducing a risky idea or recommending a novel approach may require you to take new directions. Realize how you'll need to stretch to be prepared to take action.

Know the situation. Classic business systems (think: Failure Mode and Effects Analysis) require you to assess the likelihood of failure and the potential adverse effects. You'll want to ensure you have contingency plans for actions that aren't likely to succeed and may have potentially damaging effects. Stay informed about potential risks and know the downsides involved in your choices. Your awareness is part of your resilience. You can make sense of things, improvise, and solve problems when you're in the know. Be intentional about your responses. Clarity and wise choices will contribute to your courage and your successful outcomes.

In addition, know your options. As you consider responses to situations, ensure you know multiple correct answers. If you're debating how to respond to a customer need, you may be best served to take a forceful approach that ensures your and the company's values are served. If you're seeking to sell an idea at a high-stakes meeting, you may meet with each member of the group one-on-one to garner support before you're in front of the whole group. You can express courage using a frontal approach or more nuanced strategies depending on the optimal situation.

Finally, know others. Build your social capital to build your courage. When you have a strong network of relationships, you can check in and get advice about when to take action and which actions to take. In addition, with a solid network, you will have better support if you stumble. Doing the right thing for yourself and others repeatedly builds your rapport, which will pay off when you take courageous action that may go against the grain.

Courage is also linked to resilience and adaptability. Studies show that people who practice courage are better equipped to handle stress and uncertainty. This stems from neuroplasticity, the brain's ability to rewire through experiences, which means that courageous actions can be learned and reinforced over time. Courage is a skill that can be developed through conscious effort.

Incorporating courage into daily life leads to personal growth, stronger relationships, and greater fulfillment. It helps overcome limiting beliefs, enabling individuals to pursue their dreams, stand up for themselves and others, and confidently face life's uncertainties. Courage promotes a proactive mindset, allowing individuals to embrace change and adversity as opportunities for growth.

In sum, understanding the psychology behind courage and applying it in small, consistent steps can transform our lives, leading to a more prosperous, more resilient existence.

Chapter #6

Courage And Consequences

Aria, a young woman. She was a skilled healer known for her knowledge of herbs and remedies. Her life was peaceful until one fateful day when a terrible illness began spreading through the village. People looked to her for help, but Aria was at a crossroads.

She had received an invitation from a renowned academy far away, where she could study advanced medicine, improving her skills and potentially finding a cure for the illness. But the journey was perilous—traveling through dangerous forests, leaving her village and its people behind for months. On the other hand, if she stayed in the town, she could continue treating the sick with her current knowledge, but she knew that without advanced medicine, the illness could overwhelm them all.

Both choices required immense courage. Leaving for the academy meant risking her life in an unknown world, but the reward could be her village's and many others' salvation. Staying meant facing the fear that her limited knowledge would prevent her from saving everyone. Yet, it offered the comfort of the familiar, the ability to provide immediate help, and the assurance that she was not abandoning her people.

Aria spent sleepless nights considering the consequences of both paths. If she left and failed to attend the academy, she would lose her life and leave the village without a healer. But if she succeeded, she could return stronger and save them all. On the other hand, if she stayed, she might save a few lives in the short term, but the long-term cost could be disastrous if the illness continued to spread.

Finally, after much contemplation, Aria chose to leave. While staying was the safer option, she realized the long-term risk of not gaining the knowledge to fight the disease was far more significant. She packed her belongings and set off, her heart heavy but resolute. She encountered many hardships but never lost sight of her goal. Eventually, she reached the academy, learned all she could, and returned to her village with the knowledge to heal them once and for all.

Her journey taught her that the more challenging path, though filled with uncertainties, sometimes leads to lasting change. It also revealed that true courage lies in facing immediate fears and embracing the unknown for a greater purpose.

This story highlights the importance of making decisions when faced with two challenging paths. Both paths required Aria to be brave, but she had to weigh the consequences of her choice. The lesson is that while both options may demand courage, thinking beyond the immediate fear to evaluate the long-term outcomes is crucial in making the right decision.

The key takeaway is that courage is not about the absence of fear but the ability to act despite it. When both options require bravery, it's essential to take a step back, assess the potential consequences of each path, and make a decision that aligns with your values and the future you want to create.

Aria knew that either path would bring consequences—there was no escaping that. But instead of succumbing to fear or taking the easier, more familiar route, she chose courage. She didn't run away from her fear; she faced it head-on. Despite the uncertainty and the possibility of failure, she decided to act, knowing that doing nothing or playing it safe would only prolong the inevitable.

In the end, even if her choice didn't work out as she hoped, what mattered was that she stood up to her fear, refusing to let it paralyze her. Courage doesn't guarantee success; it ensures growth, resilience, and the strength to face the next challenge.

Sometimes, we regret our actions when we fail, especially when the outcome isn't what we hoped for. But at that moment, we didn't know the consequences. Imagine if we hadn't taken action—we would have been left with a lifetime of regret for not trying.

Even if it doesn't happen as planned, taking action shows courage. At least you made a choice and faced the unknown rather than remaining paralyzed by fear. We are always given choices in life, but courage helps us create one. Courage is choosing to act, knowing that success isn't guaranteed, but growth is.

After facing pitfalls, continuing to take action is a form of courage. When you initially choose to act somewhere down the line, things might not work out as you hoped. But in those moments of failure, instead of giving up, you can pause, reassess, and start again. Reflect on how far you've come, what you've learned from each experience, and how those lessons have shaped your journey.

Moving forward depends on how you handle the fear that inevitably arises. You need courage when facing uncertainty or wanting to achieve something more significant. What happens in your mind during these moments is critical—you begin to weigh your options, face your fears, and realize that courage is about pushing through despite the unknown. It's not the absence of fear but the decision to act despite it.

When faced with a situation that requires courage, especially something new or uncertain, our minds often begin with excitement and fear. It's as if two voices emerge, each with a distinct message. One voice says, "This could go wrong, you might fail, and everyone will notice." The other voice counters, "But what if this works? What if you succeed and grow from this?"

The self-talk becomes a conversation between risk and opportunity. The doubts come first, pointing out all the reasons to hold back—fear of failure, rejection, or judgment. This voice is cautious, wanting to protect me from embarrassment or pain. It brings up past experiences where things didn't go well, trying to convince me to stay safe.

But then, there's the voice of courage. It's quieter initially but grows louder when we focus on the possibilities. This voice reminds me of times we've succeeded before, how we've overcome obstacles, and how we'll never know unless we try. It pushes us to take action, saying, "Even if you fail, you'll learn something. You'll grow."

This self-talk becomes a negotiation process, where courage isn't about ignoring fear but accepting it. It's about shifting my focus from what could go wrong to what could go right. We remind ourselves that every successful person has faced uncertainty and taken a leap of faith. Courage means understanding the 50-50 chance and still moving forward because the possibility of growth outweighs the fear of failure.

As this process continues, I feel a shift. The fear doesn't disappear, but it feels manageable. The self-talk transforms into a belief that even if things don't go perfectly, I have the strength to handle the outcome. I tell myself, "You can do this. You've done hard things before. Leap."

In the end, courage results from this ongoing conversation in my mind. It's about embracing uncertainty, trusting in my ability to adapt, and taking action despite fear. The self-talk that leads to courage isn't a one-time moment but a continuous process of reframing.

Each setback tests resilience. Courage propels you to keep going, to take action even after failure, and to trust that progress, no matter how small, is better than staying stagnant in fear.

Suppose you find yourself in a situation where you want to say "no" to something but struggle to do so. You may later regret not having had the courage to stand up for yourself, beating yourself up for not asserting your boundaries. Even though you know that saying "no" is necessary, especially if it's your first time, you may also be aware that doing so could lead to conflicts and consequences. Instead of facing those potential conflicts, you might convince yourself it's easier to avoid them by telling yourself, "It's okay, I don't have to say no," or "I can't say no," or even "I don't deserve to say no."

But if you stay in this state of avoidance, always compromising and never asserting your boundaries, you will never truly feel good about yourself. Standing up for yourself and embracing the potential conflicts of saying "no" is essential for self-respect and personal growth.

When we decide to stand up for ourselves, we must recognize that while we can control our actions, we often can't control the consequences. Both the situation and the outcomes may be challenging, but it is essential to muster the courage to choose a path and commit to it. Many of us naturally tend to avoid consequences, to run away from the problematic outcomes we fear. However, actual growth comes from facing them head-on.

When we take courage into our own hands and resolve to move forward, we open ourselves to inner dialogue. Our minds will chatter with doubts, anxieties, and uncertainties. But amidst this internal noise, we must remind ourselves to decide what we allow into our mental space. This includes choosing which thoughts to entertain and which to let go of. It's essential to calm yourself, center your thoughts, and focus on what truly matters to you.

Ultimately, it's about doing what is necessary, quieting the mind, and asking yourself: What do I want to allow into my life? What path do I want to take? Stand firm, make your choice, and move forward with confidence.

Taking action often comes with fear, and we must choose how we respond to that fear. Will you allow it to control your life, or will you take action despite it? Too often, we hesitate to act because we worry about what others might think. But the opinions of others should not dictate our choices.

When we refrain from taking action, we open ourselves to potential regret. People around us will always have differing opinions—some may commend us, while others might criticize us. Ultimately, it's essential to prioritize your values and goals over external judgments.

So, embrace your courage, take that step forward, and do what feels right. In navigating our lives, we often encounter a cacophony of opinions from those around us. People will express their thoughts in any situation, creating noise that can cloud our judgment. Each person has their own story, shaped by their experiences and perceptions, and while these narratives can offer valuable perspectives, they can also lead to confusion and self-doubt.

It's essential to recognize three narratives at play: your story, their stories, and the actual story—the reality of the situation. Among these, the most crucial is your story. This narrative defines you, your values, and your aspirations. Therefore, it's vital to take charge of your own story and identify which aspects may be holding you back from achieving your goals.

Ask yourself: What parts of your story are limiting you? Is it fear of judgment? Doubts about your abilities? Or perhaps the expectations of others? Acknowledging these barriers is the first step toward overcoming them. While it's natural for people to voice their opinions, it's essential to prioritize your desires and dreams. You must be willing to live life on your terms, even when that means diverging from the paths others expect you to take.

Choosing to live authentically requires strength and courage. It involves standing firm in your beliefs, even when faced with dissent. On the other hand, conforming to others' expectations also demands courage—it's not an easy path to take. However, it is crucial to understand that succumbing to others' narratives does not make you weak or spineless. Instead, it reflects a complex decision-making process shaped by your circumstances and values.

In the end, remember that your life is yours to lead. Embrace your story, acknowledge the noise around you, and cultivate the strength to pursue your path. Whether you forge ahead boldly or take a moment to reflect, the choice is ultimately yours. Stand tall, take control of your narrative, and let it guide you toward your goals.

Chapter #7

Leaving Comfort Zone

Courage is an essential component of living a fulfilling and authentic life. Most people live in fear, often seeking security and comfort at the cost of their true potential. This desire for security leads to stagnation, where people avoid taking risks, experiencing new things, or stepping outside their comfort zones.

Courage is the willingness to embrace uncertainty, take risks, and step into the unknown. It allows individuals to live fully in the present moment, free from the constraints of past conditioning and future anxieties. It is about saying "yes" to life and its unpredictable nature, allowing oneself to experience the joy, spontaneity, and growth that come with living dangerously.

It is important to be true to oneself, even if it means going against societal norms or expectations. True courage comes from living in alignment with one's inner self. Having the courage to be disliked means prioritizing authenticity over the approval of others. In a world where people often conform to social norms, expectations, and others' opinions, it takes courage to stand firm in who you are, what you believe, and the choices you make. When you choose to live authentically, you may face disapproval from those who disagree with you or are uncomfortable with your preferences. However, by remaining true to yourself, you experience the freedom of living in alignment with your values, not dictated by external validation.

Most people naturally desire to be liked and accepted by those around them, but constantly seeking approval can lead to a loss of self. People-pleasing often results in individuals suppressing their thoughts, desires, and ambitions to avoid conflict or criticism. Having the courage to be disliked requires breaking free from this need for approval and acknowledging that no matter what you do, there will always be people who disagree or disapprove. By letting go of the need to please everyone, you create space to pursue your passions and live more meaningfully.

Rejection and criticism are often viewed negatively, but they are an inevitable part of life. When you dare to be disliked, you understand that rejection is not necessarily a reflection of your worth but a sign that you are living authentically. It allows you to grow stronger, more resilient, and more self-assured. Criticism from others can serve

1. Be yourself: Don't try to be someone you're not. Authenticity is about embracing your true nature without apologies.

2. Drop the mask: Stop pretending to be someone you think others want you to be. This includes shedding social conditioning, expectations, and roles.

3. Embrace vulnerability: Live openly, honestly, and transparently without fear of judgment or rejection.

4. Take responsibility: Own your actions, choices, and life. Don't blame others or circumstances.

5. Live in the moment: Authenticity is about being present, not stuck in the past or worried about the future.

6. Courage is key: Living authentically requires courage, facing fears, challenges, and uncertainty.

7. Joy and danger: Living authentically brings joy but also means embracing the unknown, which can be dangerous and uncomfortable.

Remember, authenticity is a journey, not a destination. It's about embracing your true self and living with courage, honesty, and vulnerability.

Life is inherently uncertain, and attempting to control everything leads to frustration and suffering. Courage is about surrendering to the flow of life and trusting the process. It involves surrendering your need to control everything and embracing uncertainty, which can be daunting. Letting go of control requires courage because you're stepping into the unknown, where outcomes are uncertain. You're facing your fears and doubts head-on. Releasing control makes you vulnerable, which takes courage. You're opening yourself up to potential risks, mistakes, or hurt. Often, it means trusting in others, the universe, or a higher power. This trust requires courage as you believe in something beyond your control.

When you let go of control, you accept that things might not go as planned. Accepting imperfection takes courage, as you acknowledge that you can't dictate every outcome. However, it can lead to significant personal growth. You push past your comfort zone and explore new possibilities. Letting go of control is a powerful way to build courage and develop a more open, adaptable, and resilient approach to life.

Life is constantly changing, and resisting it only creates fear and anxiety. This resistance stems from our desire to remain in familiar, comfortable situations where we feel safe and in control. However, life doesn't stay the same. Circumstances shift, people evolve, and unexpected events occur. Clinging to the status quo creates inner conflict because we are fighting against the inevitable.

When we embrace change and uncertainty, we open ourselves up to opportunities for growth and transformation. Every change, even those that seem negative or challenging, brings the potential to learn, adapt, and become stronger. Uncertainty, while uncomfortable, allows us to cultivate resilience, creativity, and problem-solving skills. It pushes us out of our comfort zones, enabling personal development and deeper self-awareness.

Viewing change as a doorway to new experiences fosters a mindset of growth. Instead of fearing what's unknown, we start to see it as a chance to discover new possibilities, improve ourselves, and evolve with the flow of life. This shift in attitude reduces fear and anxiety and empowers us to face life's challenges with confidence and optimism. Embracing change transforms our perspective, helping us see life as a dynamic journey rather than something to be controlled or feared.

Samar was an ambitious young man from a middle-class family who had just completed his engineering degree. Like many in his situation, he started his career at a local company in his hometown. Though grateful for the job, Samar was determined to achieve more in life and knew he needed to explore opportunities beyond the borders of his city. However, fear and confusion held him back. The idea of stepping outside his comfort zone, away from the security of home and the familiar, weighed heavily on him. He struggled with the thought of leaving his parents, whom he had always lived with, and this attachment made it difficult for him to think about moving away for a better career.

Samar stayed in his hometown for five to six years, working hard but feeling stagnant. Despite his efforts, he wasn't growing professionally and knew he needed a change. Finally, after much contemplation, he decided to sit down with his parents and discuss his future. With their encouragement and support, Samar resolved to take a bold step forward. He realized that to grow, he had to step out of his comfort zone, take risks, and seek opportunities in other cities or countries.

Once Samar made this decision, things started to change. He began receiving job offers from different states, opening doors to possibilities he had only dreamed of. Despite his initial fear of moving to a big city and adjusting to an unfamiliar lifestyle, Samar pushed through his doubts. He reminded himself that growth requires resilience and the willingness to embrace the unknown.

Samar leaped and relocated to a new city, starting fresh. At first, he lived alone, facing the challenges of adapting to a fast-paced urban environment. But with perseverance, he soon found his footing. His hard work and determination began to pay off, and over time, he brought his parents to live with him in the new city, creating a new home together.

Looking back, Samar realized that stepping out of his comfort zone was his best decision ever. The fear of failure and the unknown was dwarfed by the progress he achieved through resilience and continuous effort. Today, Samar is thriving in his career, and his story reminds him that growth often lies on the other side of fear. For young people, Samar's journey shows that taking risks and leaving your comfort zone is essential for success. It may feel uncomfortable initially, but the rewards will come with determination.

People often become deeply accustomed to living within their comfort zone, even when they realize it may no longer serve their growth or well-being. This comfort zone, which may offer familiarity and a sense of security, can ironically become a place where they feel stuck, stagnant, and unable to move forward. Despite recognizing that they are not progressing or feeling truly fulfilled, they remain attached to this space, as stepping out into the unknown feels daunting. Though filled with dissatisfaction and even negative experiences, the comfort zone becomes a place of habitual living.

In such situations, individuals often tolerate difficulties, challenges, and discomfort because they are so used to the routine, even if it no longer brings them happiness or peace. Breaking free from societal norms, familial expectations, or other established structures can seem overwhelming. Many struggle with leaving their family environment, challenging traditional norms, or drastically changing their lives. This fear of the unknown holds them back, and they settle for a life that feels limited simply because it's familiar.

Even when faced with struggles within their comfort zone, they may convince themselves that enduring those challenges is better than facing the uncertainties that come with change. Over time, they become conditioned to accept this way of life, deriving a false sense of satisfaction from it, as it feels easier to stay where they are rather than confront the fear and effort involved in making significant changes. This cycle of habituation leads them to remain in a space that may not truly serve their personal growth or happiness but one that feels "safe" in its predictability.

People who break free from societal norms, rituals, and traditions and step out of their comfort zones are the ones who truly make progress in life. Throughout history and even in our social lives, there are countless examples of individuals who achieved greatness by challenging the status quo and venturing into the unknown. Their success was not a result of following the conventional path but rather of daring to take risks and embrace change, which led them to remarkable achievements. These individuals are now celebrated not only for their material wealth but also for their impact on society, their wisdom, and the richness they've gained in every aspect of life.

An excellent example of an international sportsperson who broke out of their comfort zone to achieve greatness is Michael Jordan, widely regarded as one of the greatest basketball players of all time. Early in his career, Jordan faced setbacks, including being cut from his high school basketball team. However, instead of staying in his comfort zone and accepting defeat, Jordan worked relentlessly to improve his skills. His tireless dedication and willingness to push himself beyond limits made him a superstar in the NBA and redefined the standards of excellence in the sport.

After achieving incredible success in basketball, Jordan took an even bolder step in 1993: He left his comfort zone to pursue a career in professional baseball. However, he faced significant challenges and was not as successful in baseball as in basketball. His willingness to leave behind his dominance in one sport to pursue a new dream showcased his courage and determination. Later, he returned to basketball and continued to achieve success, cementing his legacy as a global icon.

Another example is Serena Williams, a legendary tennis player who broke barriers on and off the court. Coming from humble beginnings, Serena and her sister Venus trained in public courts, often facing adversity and skepticism due to their background and race. Despite the challenges, Serena stepped out of her comfort zone, dominating a sport traditionally associated with affluent, predominantly white athletes. Over the years, Serena has faced injuries, setbacks, and the pressure of expectations. Yet, she continually reinvented herself, pushing her physical and mental limits to stay at the top of the game. She achieved unparalleled success in tennis and advocated for gender equality, racial justice, and body positivity, inspiring millions worldwide.

Michael Jordan and Serena Williams are prime athletes transcending their comfort zones and societal expectations. They achieved greatness through resilience, hard work, and refusing to be limited by tradition or challenges. Their stories remind us that success often requires overcoming comfort and embracing the unknown.

Throughout history, many great leaders have stepped out of their comfort zones and made significant sacrifices for the betterment of the world. Because of their courage and determination, we live in a better, more just, and more compassionate world. Leaders like Mahatma Gandhi, Abraham Lincoln, Nelson Mandela, and Mother Teresa chose to leave behind the comfort and ease of a relaxed life to address the pressing issues of their time. If they had not come forward to challenge injustice and fight for what was right, the world would not have progressed as it has today. Their legacies have shaped the freedoms and values we now enjoy.

Mahatma Gandhi left behind a comfortable life as a lawyer to fight for India's independence through non-violence. Abraham Lincoln took on the enormous challenge of abolishing slavery and preserving the Union during the American Civil War. Nelson Mandela spent 27 years in prison for standing against apartheid and racial oppression, only to emerge as the leader who would unite South Africa. Mother Teresa left the safety of her convent to serve the poorest and most vulnerable in the streets of Calcutta, dedicating her life to the service of humanity.

These leaders did not have an easy path. They faced countless challenges, hardships, and opposition. However, by breaking free from their comfort zones, they improved their lives and made the world a better place for future generations. Their actions are a powerful reminder that when you challenge your boundaries and step out of comfort, you open yourself up to more significant opportunities. While difficulties and hurdles are inevitable, overcoming them leads to personal growth and lasting impact. In doing so, you become a "shining star" for yourself and contribute to making the world better for others.

Leaving the comfort zone requires courage, which involves facing uncertainty, discomfort, and the fear of failure. However, stepping out of familiar boundaries can lead to personal growth, new opportunities, and a deeper understanding of oneself. Here are some insights into why courage is essential for leaving the comfort zone:

1. Growth Happens in Discomfort: True growth often comes from challenging situations. When you remain in your comfort zone, you limit your potential to evolve and learn new skills. Courage allows you to embrace discomfort, essential for becoming more resilient and adaptable.

2. Facing Fear: People often avoid stepping outside their comfort zones because they fear the unknown. Courage isn't the absence of fear; it's the willingness to move

forward despite it. By confronting fears, you gain confidence and realize they are not as insurmountable as they seem.

3. Opening New Opportunities: Sticking to what's familiar limits the possibilities for success, new experiences, and achievements. By taking courageous steps, you create room for unexpected opportunities that wouldn't arise otherwise. This could be in relationships, careers, or personal development.

4. Building Self-Trust: When you step outside your comfort zone, you build trust in your capabilities. Courage helps you develop the confidence to handle new challenges, reinforcing a positive cycle of taking risks and reaping rewards.

5. Expanding Horizons: Courage helps you think more broadly, push past boundaries, and explore new perspectives. It allows you to break free from routines and assumptions, opening your mind to new ways of doing things, which can lead to innovative solutions and personal breakthroughs.

6. Redefining Success: When you courageously step out of your comfort zone, you redefine success. It becomes less about avoiding failure and more about personal fulfillment and discovering what truly matters in your life.

Ultimately, leaving the comfort zone requires courage, acceptance of uncertainty, and trust in one's ability to adapt to whatever comes one's way. It's about choosing growth over complacency; the rewards often outweigh the initial discomfort.

Instead of clinging to what we already know or staying within our comfort zones, we should embrace life with a spirit of adventure. We can fully immerse ourselves in each moment by stepping out of our routines and discovering new experiences. This mindset not only enriches our own lives but also allows us to inspire those around us. By sharing our insights and encouraging others to approach life with courage, we can help them realize the abundance of embracing the unknown.

Chapter #8

Facing Your Inner Demons!

Confronting your inner demons is the first battle of success—defeat them, and the path ahead becomes clearer and brighter.

Facing your inner demons is one of the most profound acts of courage. It involves confronting fears, insecurities, past traumas, and negative thought patterns that hold you back from personal growth. This journey requires self-awareness, vulnerability, and a commitment to change, even when uncomfortable.

Ludwig van Beethoven, one of history's greatest composers, is a timeless example of how courage can help overcome inner demons. Although immense personal struggles marked his life, he transformed his pain into some of the most beautiful music ever created.

By his late 20s, Beethoven began to lose hearing, a devastating condition for a musician. By his 40s, he was almost entirely deaf. His deafness led to social withdrawal and feelings of loneliness. He often felt misunderstood and disconnected from the world around him. Beethoven struggled with depression stemming from his difficult childhood, failed relationships, and inability to hear his compositions.

After an initial period of despair, Beethoven accepted his deafness as a reality he could not change. This acceptance was the first step toward his personal growth. Beethoven learned to "hear" his music through vibrations and his exceptional imagination. He developed techniques to continue composing without relying on his ears.

Instead of giving up, Beethoven used his emotional struggles to fuel his creativity. His later works, composed during his deafness, are considered masterpieces that reflect profound emotion and resilience. Despite societal stigma and personal struggles, Beethoven continued to perform, write, and innovate, proving that courage can triumph over adversity.

Beethoven's later compositions, such as the Ninth Symphony and the "Moonlight Sonata," remain iconic and are celebrated worldwide. His ability to create extraordinary art despite immense challenges inspires countless people to overcome their struggles.

Beethoven's ability to adapt to his deafness demonstrates courage in finding new ways to achieve one's goals. Personal struggles can be a source of inspiration and creativity when channeled positively. Even in the face of seemingly insurmountable obstacles, perseverance can lead to greatness.

Misty Copeland, a world-renowned ballet dancer, overcame significant obstacles to become the first African-American female principal dancer at the American Ballet Theatre (ABT). Her journey is a story of courage, determination, and breaking societal norms.

Despite constant criticism, Misty focused on her unique strengths, realizing that her athletic build could bring something new to ballet. Misty used her platform to challenge traditional norms in ballet, proving that talent and passion are more important than race or body type. Misty worked tirelessly to perfect her craft, often practicing for hours despite financial and emotional challenges. She embraced her role as a trailblazer, inspiring young dancers from diverse backgrounds to pursue their dreams.

In 2015, Misty became the first African-American female principal dancer at ABT, a historic milestone in ballet. Misty has authored books, appeared in major campaigns, and continues to advocate for diversity in the arts.

Misty's success proves that embracing what makes you different can set you apart. Her story shows courage can break down barriers and redefine what is possible. No matter how difficult the journey, persistence, and self-belief can lead to success.

Both Beethoven and Misty Copeland demonstrate that courage is not the absence of struggle but the determination to rise above it, creating beauty and inspiration.

Inner demons are psychological constructs that reflect internal conflicts or negative emotions. Painful past experiences, such as childhood neglect or abuse, can create feelings of unworthiness or fear—negative thought patterns, like catastrophizing or self-criticism, fuel inner struggles. Societal and familial expectations can instill fear of judgment, failure, or inadequacy.

Many people try to suppress or avoid their inner demons through distractions, denial, or unhealthy coping mechanisms like overworking or substance use. However, avoidance only amplifies these issues over time.

Facing inner demons involves acknowledging their existence, understanding their origin, and addressing them directly. This requires courage and emotional resilience.

The brain's amygdala is activated when facing inner demons, triggering a fight-or-flight response. Overcoming these fears requires retraining the brain to respond with calmness and logic rather than panic.

The prefrontal cortex, responsible for self-reflection, plays a key role in understanding and analyzing one's emotions and thoughts. Increased self-awareness helps identify the root causes of inner struggles.

The brain's ability to rewire itself (neuroplasticity) allows individuals to replace negative thought patterns with positive ones. Repeatedly challenging inner demons can create healthier mental pathways over time.

Why It Takes Courage?

Looking inward can be intimidating because it exposes parts of ourselves we might not fully understand or want to acknowledge. Addressing past traumas or regrets can be emotionally taxing. Trying to change ingrained habits or beliefs comes with the possibility of setbacks, which can deter many from even starting.

Steps to Face Inner Demons

1. Self-Reflection: Identify what is holding you back (e.g., fear of failure, self-doubt, or unresolved anger).

2. Acceptance: Acknowledge these feelings or experiences without judgment.

3. Seek Help: Professional guidance from a therapist or mentor is sometimes necessary.

4. Take Action: Use strategies like journaling, meditation, or therapy to process and heal.

Facing inner demons helps overcome internal struggles and builds emotional strength, making it easier to handle future challenges. Self-reflection and emotional processing foster a deeper understanding of oneself, leading to growth and transformation. Confronting and resolving inner conflicts reduces anxiety, depression, and stress. Healing internal wounds allows individuals to connect more authentically with others.

It's a journey that requires patience, self-compassion, and perseverance. From a psychological perspective, it involves rewiring the brain to break free from fear, guilt, or doubt and fostering a mindset of resilience and empowerment. The process may be challenging, but it leads to profound personal growth and emotional liberation.

In life, achieving success, reaching our goals, fulfilling our dreams, or becoming the person we aspire to be often involves overcoming significant challenges. Among these challenges,

one of the most formidable is confronting our inner demons—
the negative thoughts, fears, doubts, and insecurities within
us. These inner demons act as obstacles, holding us back and
preventing us from taking the necessary steps toward
progress. They often create a mental barrier that makes it
difficult to move forward, regardless of whether the goal
pertains to our career, financial stability, relationships, or
personal growth.

Our inner voice, which is supposed to guide and support us,
can sometimes become our greatest enemy. It instills fear of
failure, rejection, or the unknown, making us hesitant to take
risks or try new things. This fear stems from past experiences,
societal pressures, or profoundly ingrained self-doubt. Instead
of motivating us, it paralyzes us, keeping us stuck in our
comfort zones and preventing us from reaching our true
potential.

We must learn to confront and silence our inner demons to
achieve success. This requires self-awareness, courage, and
consistent effort. By identifying the source of our fears and
understanding their root causes, we can dismantle their power
over us. Practices such as mindfulness, positive self-talk, and
seeking support from mentors or loved ones can help us build
resilience and confidence.

Ultimately, our inner demons are not invincible. They
thrive on our fears and doubts but lose their grip when we
challenge them with determination and a strong belief in
ourselves. Overcoming these internal struggles is not just
about achieving external success but also about personal

growth and self-mastery. By facing and conquering these inner battles, we pave the way for a fulfilling and meaningful life free from self-imposed limitations.

Joseph Campbell, an American writer, said, "The cave you fear to enter holds the treasure you seek." This quote symbolizes the importance of confronting our inner fears and challenges to achieve personal growth and fulfillment. It emphasizes that the most significant rewards in life often lie behind the obstacles we are most afraid to face.

Yip Man, the legendary martial artist, stated:

"We all have inner demons to fight; we call these demons fear, hatred, and anger. If you do not conquer them, a life of one hundred years is a tragedy. If you do, then a life of a single day can be a triumph."

What do you truly want in life? Do you wish to remain where you are, or do you aspire to achieve success and move forward? If you choose to advance and make progress, you must take that first courageous step.

To do so, you must silence your inner demon—the voice of fear, doubt, and hesitation—and rise above it. Overcoming this internal struggle is the key to winning the battle within yourself and taking the steps necessary to reach your goals.

The journey to success depends entirely on your courage and mindset. Every time we face a decision or a challenge, we hear two conflicting voices: one that encourages us to move forward and another—the inner demon—that instills fear and resistance. It is up to you to determine which voice you allow to guide you.

If your inner demon's voice is louder and more powerful, it can paralyze you, preventing you from taking risks or pursuing your dreams. In such a case, fear triumphs, and your progress stops.

However, if you choose to confront your inner demon with strength and determination, you can overpower it. This requires consciously listening to the voice of courage, positivity, and hope. Doing so lets you take charge of your life and move closer to success. It is not an easy task, but the choice lies in your hands: Will you allow your inner demon to control you, or will you rise above it and take control of your destiny?

Overcoming inner struggles can feel as daunting as climbing a mountain, yet with the right approach; it can become as effortless as walking on a well-lit path.

Each of us carries inner demons—negative emotions or habits that subtly influence our actions and choices, often steering us away from what's best for our mental, physical, and social well-being.

When we lose control over ourselves, we might act in ways that prioritize momentary pleasure over long-term health—like eating according to taste rather than nutritional needs—or engage in patterns that harm our mental peace or relationships. While these behaviors may not be criminal, they can profoundly affect our quality of life. No matter how deeply rooted these challenges may seem, we can win these inner battles through self-awareness, determination, and small, deliberate steps.

The first step is recognizing and understanding the emotions and behaviors that repeatedly surface, consciously or unconsciously. Once you're aware, you can start to address them through effective strategies:

1. Writing Your Thoughts:

Putting your thoughts on paper can break the repetitive, unhelpful thinking cycle. Writing helps you externalize your emotions, providing clarity and stopping you from dwelling on the same patterns.

2. Meditation:

Dedicate 15–20 minutes daily to meditation to pause and reset your thought process. This practice fosters mindfulness, giving you the strength to observe your emotions without being controlled by them.

3. Engaging in Meaningful Conversations:

Talk to someone who truly understands you—someone with experience, empathy, and the ability to offer sound advice. Their insights can help you see your struggles from a new perspective.

4. Involving Yourself in Creative or Engaging Work:

Dive into activities that inspire and interest you. Creative pursuits can help you distinguish between destructive thoughts and the present moment's reality, whether art, music, writing or another passion.

5. Practicing Gratitude:

Cultivate a habit of appreciating what you have. Gratitude shifts your focus from what's troubling you to the blessings in your life, breaking the cycle of negativity.

Every small step counts, and every effort to reclaim control over your emotions brings you closer to peace and fulfillment. Remember, no matter how fierce your inner demons may seem, they can be subdued with patience, self-awareness, and consistent action. The journey may not always be easy, but the destination—a life of balance and resilience—is worth every step.

Success is not just about external achievements; it is about winning the internal battles that often determine the course of our lives. You must defeat your inner demon, trust your abilities, and confidently take bold steps to advance. By conquering this inner struggle, you can only unlock your true potential and find the path to a fulfilling and successful life.

We are naturally imbued with courage; it is a part of who we are. However, due to social conditioning, we often become overwhelmed by fear and the boundaries set by society. These fears and limitations prevent us from realizing that courage can transform our lives. Instead, we find ourselves pleasing others, adhering to social norms, and staying within predefined boundaries, all to fit in and be accepted. But in doing so, we suppress our true selves, slowly killing the essence of who we are.

Courage can catalyze change but requires conscious effort to awaken and act upon it. Often, we witness the immense courage we possess when our loved ones or family are in need. In these moments, we find ourselves ready to face any challenge, driven by love and the desire to protect those we care about. But why do we hesitate to show the same courage toward ourselves?

Loving yourself is just as important as loving others. You must be courageous to prioritize your happiness, advocate for your well-being, and not always put yourself aside. Courage can change your life, but it is up to you to apply it to your actions. By embracing self-love and acting with courage, you can transform your life in genuinely fulfilling ways.

Chapter #9

We Can!

One day, two friends were playing near a well. One of them was 7, and the other was 8 years old. Suddenly, the older kid fell into the well. The other kid started to panic, wondering what he could do to save the drowning friend. However, he gathered himself up at such a tension and looked for ways to pull the boy out. He threw the bucket, tied a thick rope into the well, and pulled out his friend. Although the kid who fell into the well was in shock and could barely breathe, he thanked his friend for saving his life.

The most important question is, 'Where did the 7-year-old boy get the courage to save his friend's life in such a critical situation?'

A very apt answer is, ' The only reason the young kid could exhibit such velour was that no one was around him to tell him that he can't do it, to discourage him.'

Remember, 'We all have the power to do, but all it takes us is to know that we can."

Courage is an extraordinary force, often emerging within us during moments of challenge or fear when we need to protect ourselves or others. It manifests as a powerful inner strength that compels us to act, often defying limitations we once thought insurmountable. This courage is not always about grand heroic gestures; instead, it reveals itself in our everyday choices, especially when confronted by doubts or negativity from others. When someone discourages us by saying something is beyond our capability or that our efforts will be futile, courage becomes the resilience that pushes us to defy those voices, to believe in ourselves, and to persevere.

Psychologically, courage is a trait that can be nurtured from a very young age. The development of courage often starts in childhood, deeply influenced by the environment in which a child grows and the attitudes of those around them. Parents and caregivers play a significant role in this process. When a child steps into the world and begins to experience it independently, they naturally encounter situations requiring bravery. It's in these early moments that a child's understanding of courage can be shaped. When a child tries something bold or takes a risk, if parents support and encourage them rather than suppress their efforts out of fear, they foster the child's sense of courage.

The importance of this supportive environment cannot be overstated, as it instills confidence and resilience, allowing courage to flourish. Such early experiences teach a child that challenges can be faced, and fears overcome, planting the seeds of self-belief. Over time, this nurtured courage enables individuals to withstand negative influences, ignore discouraging remarks, and pursue their goals with determination. Hence, courage is not merely an innate quality; it is cultivated by encouragement, positive reinforcement, and the freedom to explore the world without excessive restraint. The ability to stand up to fear, whether internal or external, defines courage—and it is the foundation on which individuals build strength to face life's trials and pursue their dreams.

The idea that "we all have the power to do, but all it takes is to know that we can" is a profound reminder of the incredible potential within each of us. Often, we underestimate our abilities or fail to recognize the depth of our strengths simply because we lack belief in ourselves. This phrase highlights the importance of self-awareness, confidence, and the willingness to push beyond self-imposed limitations to unlock our true potential.

Every person has innate abilities, strengths, and resources, both internal and external, that equip them to achieve their goals, overcome obstacles, and adapt to new challenges. However, these qualities often lie dormant until we consciously recognize and believe in their existence. The power to achieve something remarkable or to overcome adversity is within us, but it is not enough for this power to exist—we must actively realize it. This realization acts as a catalyst, transforming potential into action. This awareness, the conscious acknowledgment of our capabilities, fuels our courage to take that first step, no matter how daunting.

Our beliefs are central to defining what we think we can achieve. When we believe we are capable, we activate a mindset of possibility, pushing us to try, persevere, and explore solutions rather than surrender to challenges. This shift in thinking can lead to resilience, determination, and creativity, empowering us to accomplish things that once seemed beyond reach. Conversely, when we doubt our abilities, we tend to avoid risks, settle for less, and miss out on opportunities that could lead to personal growth and achievement.

Moreover, knowing that we "can" is not just about having confidence; it's about cultivating a mindset that acknowledges mistakes and setbacks as part of the journey. Believing in our capacity to achieve does not mean we will always succeed easily or without failure. Instead, it means we understand that we have the resources within us to learn from failure, adapt, and try again. This self-belief becomes the cornerstone of persistence, reminding us that setbacks are temporary and that success is attainable if we are willing to keep going.

This phrase speaks to the transformative power of self-belief. We all have the potential to do great things, but conscious awareness of our abilities enables us to harness this power effectively. Once we acknowledge and embrace the belief that we can, we unlock the ability to act, grow, and achieve, transforming dreams and goals into reality.

As a child, I remember a story about a family of frogs living in a deep well. The well was home to many frogs, all accustomed to life within its dark, confined walls. However, one brave frog decided to climb the well's wall one day. Driven by curiosity or perhaps a desire for something more, he began his journey upward.

As he climbed, the other frogs looked up at him in astonishment. Soon, they began shouting and yelling, telling him to come back down. "Don't go up there," they warned. "It's dangerous!" "You'll fall!" "You won't survive the outside world!" With each step he took, the voices grew louder, filled with doubt and negativity. They told him he couldn't make it, that it was impossible, and that he was better off staying in the safety of the well.

But despite their loud warnings and discouraging words, the little frog continued climbing. He didn't look back, didn't hesitate, and didn't stop. Eventually, after much effort, he made it out of the well. As he emerged, he saw a beautiful, vast world outside—filled with sunlight, color, and boundless opportunities that he could never have imagined.

The story later revealed that the frog succeeded because he was deaf. He hadn't heard a single word of the discouragement from those below. Unable to listen to their doubts and fears, he had followed his determination and belief, reaching heights the others hadn't dared to dream of.

This story illustrates a powerful lesson: if we allow ourselves to be influenced by others' negative thoughts and doubts, we may lose sight of our potential. We believe we're incapable when we listen to voices discouraging us and may stop trying altogether. But when we trust in our abilities and stay focused on our path, we can overcome the obstacles and fears that might hold us back. Sometimes, we must tune out the negativity and listen to our courage to reach our goals and see the world beyond.

Fulfilling courage often involves building resilience, inner strength, and self-confidence. Here are some ways to nurture and fulfill your courage:

1. Face Small Fears First: Start with manageable challenges. Tackling small fears helps build courage gradually, giving you the confidence to face more significant obstacles.

2. Practice Self-Belief: Remind yourself of your strengths, accomplishments, and past successes. Self-belief is a strong foundation for courage.

3. Visualize Success: Picture yourself successfully facing your fears or challenges. Visualization can boost your confidence and make complex situations seem more achievable.

4. Seek Support: Surround yourself with people who uplift and encourage you. Having a strong support system can make you feel braver.

5. Accept Failure as a Step Forward: Understand that failure is part of growth. Instead of fearing failure, see it as a learning opportunity that makes you stronger and wiser.

6. Act with Purpose: Define your values and goals. When you're committed to something meaningful, it becomes easier to act courageously for its sake.

7. Stay Positive and Persistent. Focus on the positive outcomes of courageous actions. When challenges arise, persist and keep moving forward.

Believing in oneself is not easy. The outside world—friends, family, and others in our environment—often doubts us.

People may say we're not capable or can't achieve certain things. These doubts can affect our confidence and make self-belief even harder.

However, having the courage to believe in oneself is one of the most powerful things we can do. To clarify this concept, I want to share a real-life story about resilience and self-belief: the story of Sangram Singh, as shared by his mother, Reshmi.

Sangram Singh's journey is one of resilience and inner strength, overcoming physical challenges and skepticism from those around him. Born in a small village in Haryana, India, Sangram was diagnosed with rheumatoid arthritis at a young age, leaving him bedridden and unable to move freely. Doctors told his family that he might never walk again, and many people in his village believed that he would never be able to lead a "normal" life, let alone achieve something extraordinary.

The outer world doubted him, labeling him as a "burden" due to his disability. His relatives and even some neighbors advised his family not to invest too much hope in him, suggesting that he would never be self-sufficient. Many saw his condition as a permanent limitation, something that he and his family would have to accept. People whispered that fate already decided his life and that there was no point in dreaming beyond his physical constraints.

Amidst all these doubts and criticisms, one person refused to give up on him—his mother. She saw potential in Sangram that no one else could see. She encouraged him every day, offering her unwavering belief and love. When others suggested giving up on his future, his mother chose to help him fight back. She would carry him in her arms and help him practice simple exercises, instilling a belief that he could still rise above his physical challenges.

Her support was the spark that fuelled Sangram's determination. He practiced small movements and exercises daily, sometimes with his mother's help. Little by little, he grew stronger, pushing through the pain with the strength of his mother's encouragement. His mother remained his pillar of strength, telling him that he could accomplish anything he wanted.

Through years of relentless practice and determination, Sangram eventually regained the ability to walk, proving the doubters wrong. He set his sights on wrestling, a goal that many thought was impossible given his physical limitations. However, his mother continued to believe in him, and her support pushed him to train hard and face every challenge head-on.

Against all odds, Sangram became a champion wrestler, winning the Commonwealth Heavyweight Wrestling Championship in 2006. His journey from a child who could barely move to an international wrestling champion inspired countless people. His mother's belief in him became the foundation of his success, teaching him that sometimes, all it takes is one person's unwavering faith to overcome the world's doubts.

Sangram Singh's story reminds us of the incredible power of belief and support and how a mother's love and faith can help someone achieve the unimaginable.

Reaching our goals is often the best way to silence those who doubt us after facing rejection and negativity. The key is to believe in ourselves and stay focused on our goals without letting others' opinions sway us. We must leave their doubts and criticisms behind, dedicating ourselves to continuous self-improvement and forward movement. This journey requires courage, but when we truly believe in ourselves, that courage comes naturally.

Remember, courage is a muscle that can be developed and strengthened with practice, self-reflection, and support from others.

Ashima Sen is an example of people losing hope when thinking about anything.

It was 2011; she was traveling by train to take an exam. More than three robbers started to loot valuable items. The brave girl resisted the robbers, and while the train was at 80Kmph, she was pushed out. Immediately, as she fell on the railway track, another train on a parallel track crushed her leg below the knee.

Both legs were in pieces, and for many hours, no one came to the rescue. Crows were eating the muscles of the affected part. Compare how we feel if we get a small cut in our body. I can't imagine how much pain she was facing at that instant.

Later, she was admitted to the hospital, where the team of doctors wasn't able to save both her legs. ...

Exactly two years ago, she climbed Mount Everest with a prosthetic leg. On 21 May 2013, she stepped on her legs to climb for 52 days.

She said, "I wanted to tell everyone that I'm on top of the world, especially to those people who thought a woman and an amputee couldn't do it."

"Agar ye ho sakta hai na, toh kuch bhi ho sakta hai "(if this would be possible then, nothing is impossible).

When faced with unfavorable situations, people typically have two options: blame their circumstances, feel victimized, and wallow in sadness, or rise and confront the problem with strength. Instead of succumbing to despair, they can declare, "I am stronger than this, and I will overcome you."

Embracing courage allows individuals to take proactive steps toward their goals. Once our mindset shifts to one of determination, courage follows, empowering us to pursue our ambitions. Regardless of our burdens, blockages, or hurdles, we can overcome them.

By choosing the path of courage, we focus on our goals. In pursuit of these objectives, we confront and navigate challenges, drawing strength from within to overpower obstacles. Ultimately, this mindset and courage enable us to achieve what we desire.

Chapter #10

Victory Is Yours!

In an evening of unexpected twists and relentless battles, Juventus faced RB Leipzig in Germany and emerged with a story of resilience despite a cascade of setbacks. For the Italian side, this was more than just a game; it was a testament to their tenacity, courage, and never-say-die spirit under coach Thiago Motta.

The match was barely four minutes in when Lois Openda quickly brushed past Gleison Bremer, setting up an immediate chance for Leipzig. Defender Pierre Kalulu's desperate clearance barely kept Juventus in the game, but Bremer wasn't so lucky. Twisting his ankle and knee during the challenge, the Brazilian had to exit, leaving his team shaken and bringing Federico Gatti off the bench.

Just as Juventus attempted to settle, another blow struck: Nico Gonzalez began showing signs of a thigh injury. Francisco Conceicao stepped in, yet Juve had already expended two of their substitution slots within 12 minutes of play—a costly setback with much of the game still to go.

And then, the breakthrough came for Leipzig. Another brilliant ball from Openda connected with Benjamin Sesko, who delivered a powerful strike off the crossbar, scoring the first goal conceded by Juventus this season.

Fighting from behind, Juventus found another setback when Castello Lukeba's tackle on Dusan Vlahovic was reviewed by VAR, with no penalty awarded. Yet Motta's team pressed on, hoping for a break. Teun Koopmeiners hit the post early in the second half, signaling Juve's determination to turn things around.

Moments later, Andrea Cambiaso sent a precise ball into the box, allowing Vlahovic to find the net and reignite Juventus' hope. But Leipzig quickly countered with Openda bursting forward. When Juventus goalkeeper Michele Di Gregorio came out of his area to confront him, the ball appeared to graze his gloves. VAR confirmed the infraction, and Di Gregorio was sent off, leaving Juventus to play with 10 men.

Substitute Douglas Luiz had barely entered the game when he conceded a penalty for a handball while trying to shield his face from the powerful free-kick. Sesko's penalty kick slid into the net, giving Leipzig a two-goal lead and seeming to seal Juventus' fate.

Down to 10 players and facing an uphill battle, Juventus didn't give up. Vlahovic capitalized on an opportunity to curl a remarkable shot into the top corner, tightening the score and proving that the Bianconeri's fighting spirit was alive. The two teams exchanged blows, and in the 83rd minute, Conceicao struck with a breathtaking goal that once again put Leipzig ahead.

Juventus showed relentless effort and cohesion despite being a man down, defying their numerical disadvantage.

Coach Motta praised his team's resilience, noting, "The key word was courage. Courage from the boys determined to get forward to cause problems for the opposition."

If one player personified Juve's spirit that night, it was Nicolo Fagioli. Building on an excellent performance against Genoa, Fagioli commanded the midfield with unrelenting energy and precision. SofaScore stats show his effectiveness: 7 duels won, a remarkable 98% pass completion (62 of 63 attempts), and a critical assist on Conceicao's goal.

Fagioli reflected on the match, "Maybe it wasn't a perfect match, but certainly a great one: maybe the best since I've been here, and it all starts now. I'm giving everything to get better and better."

Ultimately, it may not have been a flawless performance, but Juventus' resilience brought them another three points. Motta's side will return to domestic competition, where they'll need to channel this same relentless energy to keep pace with Serie A leaders Napoli.

It was a night when little went Juventus' way. Yet, thanks to players like Fagioli and Vlahovic, the Bianconeri came away with much more than just points—they showed a renewed spirit and determination that could be vital as they push forward this season.

This story clearly illustrates that courage is essential to reaching our goals in any part of life. When we find the strength to face challenges head-on, we open the door to success. Achieving something through courage brings happiness beyond words, a feeling that lifts us above the ordinary and fills us with a deep sense of accomplishment and joy.

Courage is often the invisible force that can turn the tide when everything seems lost—in Juventus' recent clash with RB Leipzig, the Italian side faced adversity on nearly every front. Yet, they summoned incredible bravery that kept them in the game and redefined the outcome. This game provided a powerful example of how courage—fuelled by belief, resilience, and unity—can change the course of events, even when the odds seem overwhelmingly against you.

1. Courage to Overcome Early Setbacks

Juventus' night in Germany started disastrously. Within minutes, they lost two key players to injury, used up two valuable substitution slots, and conceded a goal. For many teams, such an inauspicious beginning would have shattered morale, causing players to lose focus and confidence. But Juventus didn't allow these setbacks to define them. Instead, they rallied. Coach Thiago Motta's unwavering belief in his players instilled the courage they needed to keep fighting despite their weakened state. Their commitment to push forward, even when down, showed their collective courage to continue striving against a powerful opponent.

2. Resilience in the Face of Bad Luck and Injustice

When Michele Di Gregorio, Juventus' goalkeeper, was sent off, and Douglas Luiz conceded a penalty almost immediately after, the situation seemed hopeless. Many teams would have accepted defeat down to 10 men, trailing further behind. Yet Juventus demonstrated immense resilience, fuelled by courage, choosing not to give up. The players stepped up their game, matching Leipzig's intensity and attacking with tenacity, refusing to allow their circumstances to define them. Courage meant daring to push for a goal even when numerical disadvantage and fatigue were stacked against them.

3. Courage as the Catalyst for Change

What made Juventus' courage transformative was its ability to reignite hope and drive results. Nicolo Fagioli, who exemplified this courage, became a central figure in the midfield, dominating with his passing accuracy and tenacity. When Dusan Vlahovic scored his stunning goal, it symbolized a shift in the scoreboard and the players' mentality—an understanding that the game was far from over. Juventus' courageous comeback efforts helped them regain momentum and put Leipzig on the defensive, proving that courage can inspire, lead, and fuel players to achieve what seems improbable.

4. Courage as a Reflection of Team Spirit and Unity

Courage doesn't just live within individuals; it is a collective force that draws strength from unity. Juventus' players demonstrated how courage can unify a team, driving each member to give their best despite their daunting obstacles. Motta's post-match comments highlighted this, emphasizing the courage that "the boys showed...to be proactive, to play good football...even with a man down." This unity under pressure transformed Juventus from a defeated team into a determined force. Their collective courage allowed them to fight as individuals and as one cohesive unit, pushing Leipzig to their limits.

5. Courage as a Game Changer

This match was proof that courage is a potent game-changer. In sports, victories don't always come from having the best players or tactics; they come from the will to press on, take risks, and pursue opportunities, even when failure seems imminent. Courage was the fuel that allowed Juventus to fight back, close the gap, and come tantalizingly close to a comeback. Though Leipzig ultimately won, Juventus left with their heads held high, knowing that courage had allowed them to challenge and shape the game on their terms.

Courage transformed a challenging night into a display of what Juventus could achieve, even under adverse conditions. It reminded everyone watching that bravery in the face of setbacks can change outcomes, shifting narratives from failure to heroism. As Juventus returns to Series A, their courage in this match will likely continue to define them, turning them into a formidable force, ready to chase success regardless of obstacles.

When people passively accept a challenging situation without taking action to address it, they may already feel defeated. By convincing themselves they lack the courage or strength to face it, they set a mindset of failure before even trying. This mindset can prevent them from moving forward and achieving their potential.

To overcome this, we must tap ourselves to take meaningful steps forward. Doing so transforms our approach to challenges, opening up the possibility of victory and success. With courage, no obstacle is insurmountable, and the path to achievement becomes attainable. Into their inner courage and confront the situation with determination. Courage doesn't mean being fearless; it means facing challenges despite the fear. When we find and cultivate that inner strength, we empower ourselves to take meaningful steps forward. Doing so transforms our approach to challenges, opening up the possibility of victory and success. With courage, no obstacle is insurmountable, and the path to achievement becomes attainable.

We embrace courage and decide to face a situation head-on, committing to overcome it no matter what. Our minds and bodies align with this determination. This decision sends a powerful signal to our brain, preparing it to handle challenges with resilience. This mental shift energizes us, often providing a surge of strength and focus that enhances our ability to act effectively.

With every courageous step, each action we take becomes a building block toward victory. Whether in sports, our careers, or personal situations at home, we approach challenges with courage and set ourselves up for success. Courage enables us to tackle difficulties with a proactive mindset, turning obstacles into opportunities for growth. With this unwavering resolve, victory becomes a possibility and a natural outcome of our determination.

"Courage is equal to victory" captures a profound truth about the human experience. While victory in any endeavor—sports, personal challenges, or professional pursuits—often requires skill, strategy, and hard work, courage ultimately serves as the foundation for success.

Victory rarely comes without a willingness to take risks. Courage is the driving force that prompts individuals to step outside their comfort zones and confront challenges. Whether facing a formidable opponent in a sports match, pursuing a career goal, or navigating personal hardships, courage propels us to take the necessary actions. Without it, even the most skilled individuals may remain stagnant and hesitant to act due to fear of failure or rejection.

It often involves overcoming obstacles and setbacks. Courage enables individuals to persevere through difficulties, maintaining focus and determination despite challenges. When faced with adversity, those who possess courage are more likely to push through, learn from their experiences, and adapt their strategies. This resilience fosters growth and improvement, ultimately leading to a higher likelihood of success.

Courage alters our mindset. When we face our fears and tackle situations boldly, we see opportunities rather than limitations. This shift in perspective allows us to approach challenges with optimism and creativity, opening doors that may have seemed closed. A courageous mindset fosters innovation and resourcefulness, enabling us to find solutions that lead to victory.

Courageous actions empower individuals. Each step in the face of fear reinforces a belief in one's abilities and potential. This empowerment not only boosts self-confidence but also encourages further courageous actions. As individuals experience victories—no matter how small—they build momentum that fuels their drive to face even more significant challenges. This cycle of courage leading to action and action leading to victory creates a powerful positive feedback loop.

Courage is contagious. When individuals demonstrate bravery in facing challenges, they often inspire those around them to do the same. This collective courage can create a supportive environment where everyone feels empowered to strive for victory. In team settings, whether in sports or work, this shared courage fosters collaboration and unity, enhancing the overall chances of success.

Finally, it's essential to recognize that external achievements do not solely define victory. While winning a game or receiving a promotion are tangible successes, true victory often lies in personal growth and resilience. The courage to confront fears, learn from failures, and continue striving for improvement can be seen as victories in themselves. In this sense, courage becomes synonymous with pursuing excellence, growth, and fulfillment.

Equating courage with victory is not an exaggeration; it reflects the essence of what it means to succeed. Courage ignites action, fosters resilience, empowers individuals, inspires others, and shapes what victory means. By embracing courage, we equip ourselves with the tools necessary to navigate life's challenges and emerge victorious in our endeavors, whatever they may be.

The excellent book Bhagavad Gita, one of the most revered texts in Indian philosophy and spirituality, presents profound teachings on navigating life's complexities, particularly when faced with challenges. At its core, the Gita emphasizes the importance of courage, determination, and the rejection of cowardice as essential virtues for personal growth and fulfillment.

The Bhagavad Gita is set during a great war. Prince Arjuna is torn between his duty as a warrior and his moral dilemmas about fighting against his kin. As he stands on the battlefield, he is overwhelmed with doubt and fear, contemplating the consequences of the war. In this moment of crisis, Lord Krishna, who serves as Arjuna's charioteer and spiritual guide, imparts wisdom that addresses the nature of courage and the necessity of facing life's challenges.

One of the key teachings of the Gita is that courage is not merely the absence of fear but the ability to act despite fear. Lord Krishna encourages Arjuna to rise above his doubts and insecurities, reminding him of his responsibilities and duties as a warrior. This call to action illustrates that true courage involves recognizing one's responsibilities and facing them with resolve. The Gita teaches one to confront challenges head-on rather than succumb to fear or inaction.

Determination is another crucial aspect highlighted in the Gita. Krishna urges Arjuna to focus on his duty (dharma) as a warrior and not be swayed by emotions or the outcomes of his actions. This idea reinforces the importance of steadfastness and commitment to one's path, regardless of possible difficulties. Maintaining a determined mindset allows individuals to push through challenges and emerge stronger.

The Gita categorically denounces cowardice as a barrier to personal growth and fulfillment. Cowardice is portrayed as a refusal to engage with life's challenges and an avoidance of one's responsibilities. Lord Krishna emphasizes that succumbing to fear leads to stagnation and regret. By framing cowardice in this manner, the Gita inspires individuals to embrace their inner strength and confront their trials rather than retreating into complacency.

A central theme of the Gita is the journey towards self-realization and understanding one's true nature. Krishna teaches that individuals can cultivate the strength needed to face challenges by connecting with the inner self. This inner strength is rooted in recognizing one's eternal soul (atman) and its connection to the divine. When individuals realize their true nature, they find the courage to confront adversity, knowing they are part of something greater.

It also emphasizes the principle of performing actions without attachment to the results. Krishna advises Arjuna to act according to his duty without being influenced by the fear of success or failure. This approach encourages a focus on the process rather than the outcome, fostering a courageous mindset that allows individuals to engage fully in their actions. When people act with this sense of detachment, they free themselves from the paralyzing effects of fear and anxiety, thus empowering them to tackle challenges more effectively.

The teachings of the Bhagavad Gita extend beyond the context of Arjuna's dilemma; they serve as a universal guide for humanity. In today's fast-paced and often unpredictable world, individuals face many personal, professional, and societal challenges. The Gita's message resonates strongly, encouraging people to harness their courage and determination to navigate these complexities. By doing so, individuals can cultivate resilience, embrace change, and strive for personal and collective growth.

The Bhagavad Gita imparts invaluable lessons on the significance of courage and determination in facing life's challenges. It teaches that cowardice is unacceptable and detrimental to one's growth and fulfillment. By embracing courage, individuals can fulfill their responsibilities, engage with life authentically, and ultimately find strength and wisdom in the face of adversity. The Gita is a timeless reminder that we can transcend our limitations and achieve our highest potential through courage and determination.

Courage is profoundly exemplified in any country's armed forces. Soldiers embody extraordinary bravery and unwavering determination in their commitment to duty. They are often willing to make the ultimate sacrifice of their lives for the safety and security of their nation. This selflessness and resolve highlight the essence of courage, demonstrating that true valor involves the willingness to face danger and dedication to a more significant cause.

The armed forces serve as a powerful example for all of us, reminding us that courage is not just about physical strength but also mental fortitude and a sense of responsibility. These individuals undergo rigorous training, often in life-or-death situations, preparing themselves to confront formidable challenges. Their willingness to step forward despite overwhelming odds inspires us to cultivate similar qualities.

We can learn from the courage displayed by military personnel and apply those lessons to our daily experiences. Whether in our careers, personal relationships, or community engagements, embracing courage allows us to confront challenges head-on and diligently pursue our goals. The values of bravery, commitment, and sacrifice demonstrated by soldiers are a powerful reminder that when we approach life with courage, we can overcome obstacles and make a meaningful impact in our spheres of influence.

The courage ordinary citizens display when facing daily struggles and challenges is equally significant. Each person, regardless of age or gender—be it a child, woman, man, or elder—encounters obstacles that require courage to confront. Whether overcoming personal difficulties, standing up for what is right, or simply navigating the complexities of daily responsibilities, facing these challenges head-on is commendable.

Every small step taken with courage contributes to personal growth and can positively influence the community around us. Courage is not limited to grand acts of heroism; it is found in the determination to rise above adversity and take action, no matter how small. Individuals can foster resilience and inspire others by choosing not to succumb to cowardice and instead actively engaging with life's challenges.

When everyone in society embraces courage, it creates a ripple effect that enhances the community as a whole. A courageous person is often a source of inspiration, motivating others to take similar steps towards improvement. Thus, cultivating courage within ourselves and encouraging it in others can lead to a better, more supportive, and progressive society. Each act of bravery, no matter how minor it may seem, deserves recognition and appreciation, as it plays a vital role in shaping a stronger, more resilient community.

Chapter #11

Small Actions!

Whether it's a military victory, artistic achievement, social activism, or entrepreneurial success, courage is the foundation for any significant accomplishment. However, this does not mean courage is reserved for a select few or unattainable for others. Courage is a quality that we can all cultivate. It is through acts of courage that we achieve greatness in life. But it is equally important to demonstrate small acts of courage in our everyday lives. These small steps build the strength and confidence to face significant challenges and accomplish remarkable things.

In May 1940, during the early stages of World War II, Allied forces were outflanked by the German army in France, leading to a massive retreat to the beaches of Dunkirk. The situation was dire, with around 400,000 British and Allied troops trapped, facing annihilation or capture.

The British government and military, anticipating the possibility of such a catastrophic situation, preemptively prepared for emergency evacuations. Naval officers, engineers, and civilian volunteers collaborated to organize Operation Dynamo, a large-scale rescue effort.

The British also leveraged a strategic psychological preparation by maintaining morale among troops and civilians. Civilians with boats were informed in advance and ready to assist, while military commanders kept the soldiers calm under immense pressure.

Thanks to this preparation, the evacuation succeeded beyond expectations. Between May 26 and June 4, 1940, over 338,000 troops were safely evacuated from Dunkirk. Although it was still a significant blow, the damage was far less than if the British had been unprepared. The troops saved at Dunkirk played a critical role in the war's later stages, demonstrating how preparedness for a shock mitigates its consequences.

This event is often called the "Dunkirk Spirit," symbolizing resilience and readiness in adversity.

Unprepared for a shock causes the most damage. By anticipating the outcome of any problem and working on its solution beforehand, we can stay alert and ready.

And you can face the danger more quickly. It's not necessary that thinking about your fears will make you a billionaire, but when you understand your worries well, their intensity diminishes. And whenever such a time comes, you are ready to face it.

Courage can be built through small efforts. Whenever we imagine a courageous act, a vast image of barriers to facing dangers comes to our mind. Then we think of a citizen or someone who refuses to bow down before oppressors.

Sometimes courage indeed looks magnificent, but not always. Often, doing small and very ordinary tasks also requires courage. Aristotle believed that virtues are things we can achieve day by day.

Mastery of any task is not achieved in a single day but through small, consistent efforts every day. Similarly, to become brave, one should perform small acts of courage from time to time. Every big thing starts small, so you don't need to do something grand in the name of courage.

Florence Nightingale, often called "The Lady with the Lamp," is a timeless example of how small, courageous steps can lead to monumental change.

Born into a wealthy English family in 1820, Florence was expected to live a conventional life of luxury. However, she felt a deep calling to serve others, particularly in the nursing field—a profession then considered lowly and unsuitable for women of her status. Her decision to pursue nursing was her first courageous step, defying societal norms and her family's expectations.

Despite opposition from her family, Florence began training as a nurse in Germany. She learned basic medical care and sanitary practices, laying the foundation for her future work. This small yet bold step began her dedication to improving healthcare.

Florence became a symbol of hope as she made her nightly rounds with a lamp in hand, checking on patients. This simple act of compassion showed that courage isn't always grand; it's often about consistently showing up, even in the face of adversity.

Florence Nightingale's life teaches us that small, courageous steps—taken with determination and purpose— can lead to extraordinary change. Her journey proves that true bravery lies in persistence, not grand gestures.

Sometimes, one should not miss the chance to take a practical start, no matter how small it may be. Courage journeys from a confident start to true bravery. However, it is also important not to linger around small things too long. Thomas Edison said life is too short to stay stuck on small things for too long. He always gravitated toward challenging tasks.

However, if your courageous steps are small, there is no need to worry. But these steps only matter if they are taken in the right direction. So, show your courage in the field where it truly matters. Start small, but also decide that you will achieve something big one day.

One significant incident in Chhatrapati Shivaji Maharaj's life, where a decisive step had a considerable impact, was the Capture of Torna Fort in 1645.

At just 16, Shivaji Maharaj led his first major military campaign to capture Torna Fort in the Western Ghats' Sahyadri range. The fort was strategically important and under the control of the Bijapur Sultanate at the time.

Shivaji and his small force of men scaled the steep and challenging terrain, taking the fort from the Bijapur forces without much resistance. The entire operation was executed quickly and decisively. It was a critical moment for Shivaji, as it marked the beginning of his military career and his campaign to establish an independent Maratha kingdom.

This quick and bold action laid the foundation for Shivaji's future campaigns, inspiring his followers and demonstrating his leadership and strategic acumen. The capture of Torna Fort was the first of many such victories, expanding his kingdom and ultimately leading to the establishment of the Maratha Empire.

In this instance, Shivaji's decisive action in taking a fort at such a young age, with minimal resources, showed his strategic brilliance and determination, which would define his legacy as a warrior king.

Though capturing Torna Fort was a small step in the grand scheme, it laid the foundation for Shivaji's larger goal of Swarajya—an independent rule free from foreign domination. It set the stage for many more such victories, expanding Shivaji's influence and ultimately leading to the establishment of the Maratha Empire.

In this way, the small step of capturing Torna Fort was the starting point of Shivaji Maharaj's relentless pursuit of Swarajya. This vision would unite and empower the people of India to assert their independence.

Sometimes, it takes a few moments to muster the courage to take action. You need to take that first step. Once you've decided, you begin moving in that direction, no matter how small the task may be. Whether making a simple phone call, sending an email, or even just saying something to someone, each action reflects your courage.

Heroism is the courage shown for others. Many stories in history depict heroism. Even daily, we often witness people showing courage for others. In those moments, we see them as our heroes.

Rani Durgavati was a brave and wise queen who ruled the kingdom of Gondwana in the 16th century. External forces, including the Mughal Empire, often threatened her kingdom. One day, the Mughal emperor, Akbar, sent his forces to invade Gondwana. Rani Durgavati's son, Vir Narayan Singh, went into battle alongside his mother and the kingdom's army to protect her kingdom and people.

The Mughal forces, however, were overpowering, and the situation became dire. Rani Durgavati, realizing that the only way to ensure the survival of her people and the future of her kingdom was to offer a great sacrifice, made an extraordinary decision. She knew her son, the rightful heir, could be saved by providing a strategic concession.

To protect the life of the king's son and ensure the long-term survival of her people, she made the heart-wrenching decision to sacrifice her own son's life. This selfless act was driven by their love for her kingdom and her duty as a mother and ruler, as she put the well-being of her people over her grief.

Like many others in history, this story exemplifies the ultimate sacrifice a mother can make—putting her child's life aside for a more significant cause. It highlights the profound depth of love, sacrifice, and heroism that can arise under challenging circumstances.

Was it easy for her? Certainly not. At that moment, her mind must have been overwhelmed with turmoil. She had two choices: she could save herself and her son, or she could choose to save her kingdom and her people. But she gathered the courage to make the unimaginable decision to sacrifice her son for the greater good of her people and her kingdom. It was undoubtedly a tough choice, but she made it. This act epitomizes courage, requiring an intense mindset and resolve.

Sometimes, we must muster the courage to let go of what we have invested everything in. If we don't, we can suffer significant losses. This requires a lot of courage, but one does not gain fame or recognition in return. Self-sacrifice for the benefit of others is called heroism.

Bhagat Singh, a young revolutionary from Indian history, embodied unparalleled courage. His love and dedication to his country's freedom were so profound that he boldly challenged the British colonial regime when most young men were concerned with their futures. In an audacious act, he threw a bomb into the British Assembly, aiming to awaken the nation's conscience. Though he was arrested and later sentenced to death, he accepted his fate with remarkable composure and without regret. Bhagat Singh's courage was not just in his actions but also in his unwavering commitment to his cause, making his bravery beyond words and truly extraordinary. His sacrifice continues to inspire generations, demonstrating a level of courage that is both rare and awe-inspiring.

Sometimes, you can inspire others through your actions, even with just your words. This, too, is called heroism. People are often willing to do anything for the words of their hero. When a hero speaks, whether it is a call for sacrifice or a call to take action in life, their words hold such power and influence that they inspire deep devotion. The hero's conviction, passion, and belief in a cause resonate so strongly with others that it sparks a willingness to follow, even at a high personal cost. The hero symbolizes courage, strength, and determination, and their words become a guiding light, motivating people to take bold steps, make sacrifices, and embrace challenges. This profound connection and trust in the hero's vision drives individuals to do whatever it takes, often going beyond their limits, to live up to their hero's expectations and ideals.

When the Persian Empire, led by King Xerxes, invaded Greece with an enormous army, the Greek city-states united to defend their homeland. The narrow pass at Thermopylae, located between the mountains and the sea, became the chosen battleground. King Leonidas of Sparta, known for his courage and leadership, led a small force of 300 Spartans and several thousand Greek allies to hold off the massive Persian army.

"It is not the number of soldiers, but the spirit of the warrior that wins the battle." – This sentiment reflects Leonidas' belief in the strength of his warriors' hearts over the size of the enemy's forces.

Leonidas and his men fought bravely, knowing their sacrifice was essential for Greece's survival. The battle lasted three days, and the Spartans' courage inspired the rest of the Greek forces. Their strategic positioning at Thermopylae allowed the Greeks to inflict significant losses on the Persian army.

However, the Spartans knew they could not win this battle due to the overwhelming numbers of the Persians. Despite this, Leonidas and his men chose to make the ultimate sacrifice. They held the pass long enough to give the other Greek forces time to retreat and prepare for future battles. Leonidas and his 300 Spartans fought to the death, demonstrating incredible bravery and selflessness.

Their heroic stand symbolized courage, honor, and the willingness to sacrifice for the greater good. Even though they lost the battle, their actions eventually inspired the Greeks to defeat the Persians, culminating in the famous Battle of Plataea the following year.

The story of King Leonidas and the 300 Spartans is a timeless example of heroism. Bravery and sacrifice for the more significant cause transcend the immediate consequences. It is a tale of how courage and honor can leave an indelible mark on history, even in the face of inevitable defeats.

Being courageous means facing challenges with happiness and being willing to put your reputation and livelihood at stake when necessary. It doesn't mean fear; instead, it means defining and managing that fear.

The examples of courage we see in history are often glorious and grand. However, that was not always the case, at least not initially. Sometimes, taking the proper steps, making phone calls, sending emails, or expressing your opinion can be courageous. Often, when a person in society performs an act of bravery, society doesn't readily accept them.

Kailash Satyarthi is an Indian child rights activist who worked to end child labor and exploitation. Born in a village in India, he faced significant resistance from the local communities when he began his fight against child labor. Villagers often saw him as challenging traditional practices, and his efforts were met with suspicion and hostility. Despite this, his bravery led to the establishment of Bachpan Bachao Andolan, an organization that has rescued thousands of children from exploitative conditions. Over time, his work gained global recognition, eventually earning him the Nobel Peace Prize in 2014, but initially, he faced significant opposition and rejection from those around him.

Medha Patkar is an activist who worked against the Narmada Valley Project. A resident of a village in India, she stood up against the displacement of rural communities caused by the construction of dams in the region. Many in her village and surrounding areas initially resisted her activism, viewing it as threatening their economic growth. Despite facing harsh criticism and even threats, her courage sparked a movement that challenged large-scale development projects in rural India, highlighting how acts of bravery can often face initial rejection in village societies.

So, don't expect everyone to welcome your courageous steps. Don't do anything for applause or reward, at least not initially. You may have to face loneliness in the beginning. The idea here is that you should take courageous steps based on your values, beliefs, and desires rather than seeking approval or rewards from others. This type of motivation is often associated with higher satisfaction and long-term persistence.

When someone courageously challenges societal norms or expectations, they may experience social rejection or isolation, especially in the early stages. People may resist new ideas or behaviors, particularly if they disrupt the status quo. This can lead to feelings of loneliness or exclusion, a common psychological experience when one's actions are not immediately accepted or understood by others.

To navigate the challenges, reflect deeply on what truly matters to you. Understand the reasons why you're taking courageous steps independent of external approval. A strong connection to your intrinsic motivations helps you stay grounded when facing resistance. Seek out those who share your values or who support personal growth. Surrounding yourself with people who understand your journey can provide emotional validation and lessen feelings of isolation.

Keep cultivating the growth mindset by viewing challenges, setbacks, and loneliness as learning opportunities. Ask yourself, "What can I learn from this experience?" It becomes easier to endure when you approach discomfort with curiosity and openness.

Transformation, whether personal or societal, often takes time. Understand that the changes you're trying to make may not be immediately visible or appreciated, but persistence will lead to growth and eventual acceptance. Keep pushing forward even when things seem difficult.

Be kind to yourself when facing rejection or isolation. Self-compassion helps you stay resilient. Acknowledge that setbacks do not reflect your failure but are part of the human experience.

Visualize how your actions align with your values and will ultimately contribute to your growth and well-being. This can motivate you and keep you focused on the long-term rewards of following your path.

Journaling, meditation, or self-reflection can help you stay connected to your intrinsic motivations and process the emotions of rejection or isolation. This can keep you emotionally grounded and help you maintain perspective.

Here are some well-known exercises and strategies to cultivate courage in behavior:

1. Exposure Therapy

What It Is: Gradually exposing yourself to your fears or challenging situations.

How to Practice:

Identify something you fear but want to overcome (e.g., public speaking).

Start with small steps, such as speaking in front of a trusted friend, and gradually move to larger audiences.

2. The "Worst-Case Scenario" Exercise

What It Is: Imagining the worst possible outcome of a situation to reduce fear.

How to Practice:

Write down the worst thing that could happen in a situation.

Reflect on how you would handle it and realize it's often not as bad as it seems.

3. Daily Acts of Bravery

What It Is: Taking small, intentional risks every day.

How to Practice:

Start a conversation with a stranger.

Speak up in a meeting or classroom.

Try something new, like a hobby or food.

4. Power Posing (Amy Cuddy's Research)

What It Is: Adopting confident body language to influence your mindset.

How to Practice:

Stand in a "power pose" (e.g., hands on hips, chest out) for 2 minutes before a challenging task.

5. Journaling About Fear and Courage

What It Is: Reflecting on your fears and acts of courage.

How to Practice:

Write about situations where you lacked courage and analyze why.

Note moments when you showed courage and how it made you feel.

6. The "3-Second Rule"

What It Is: Taking action within 3 seconds of thinking about it.

How to Practice:

If you want to approach someone, count to three and do it before overthinking.

7. Visualization

What It Is: Mentally rehearsing courageous actions.

How to Practice:

Close your eyes and visualize yourself confidently handling a challenging situation.

8. Practice Gratitude for Courageous Moments

What It Is: Reflecting on courageous acts you or others have done.

How to Practice:

Write down three courageous things you did in the past week.

9. Stoic Exercises (Inspired by Stoic Philosophy)

What It Is: Preparing for difficulties by imagining them.

How to Practice:

Practice "negative visualization" by imagining challenges you might face and how you would respond.

10. Affirmations for Courage

What It Is: Repeating positive statements to reinforce courage.

How to Practice:

Use affirmations like "I am brave and capable of handling challenges" daily.

11. Cold Showers or Similar Challenges

What It Is: Facing discomfort to build resilience and courage.

How to Practice:

Take a cold shower or do an activity that makes you uncomfortable for a short time.

12. Join Courage-Building Activities

Examples:

Take an improved class to overcome stage fear.

Join a group like Toastmasters to build public speaking courage.

These exercises work gradually, helping you develop courage as a habit over time. Which one would you like to try?

Fear setting Listing

Define: List the worst things that could happen

1

____

____

2

____

____

3

____

____

4

____

____

5

____

____

6

____

____

7

8

9

10

Prevent: List how you can stop the above bad things

1

2

3

4

5

____

____

6

____

____

7

____

____

8

____

____

9

____

____

10

____

____

Repair: If the worst happens, list how to repair each bad thing.

1

____

____

2

____

____

3

____

____

4

____

____

5

____

____

6

____

____

7

____

____

8

____

____

9

____

____

10

____

____

Benefits: List all possible benefits from taking this action

1

____

____

2

____

____

3

____

____

4

____

____

5

____

____

6

____

____

7

____

____

8

9

10

6 Months: List the costs of inaction during this time

1

2

3

4

5

1 Year: List the costs of inaction during this time

1

____

____

2

____

____

3

____

____

4

____

____

5

____

____

3 Years: List the costs of inaction during this time

1

____

____

2

____

____

3

____

____

4

____

____

5

____

____

★★★

"Courage is what it takes to stand up and speak; courage is also what it takes to sit down and listen."

- Winston Churchill

"Be brave, leap, and watch the universe conspire to make your dreams a reality."

– Rumi.

"Courage is resistance to fear, mastery of fear, absence of fear. Except a creature is part coward, it is not a compliment to say it is brave; it is merely a loose misapplication of the word."

- Mark Twain

"Courage is not believing something despite the evidence but the courage to do something regardless of the consequences."

Disclaimer

The information provided in this book is for educational and informational purposes only. The author and publisher do not offer medical, psychological, legal, or financial advice, and the content should not be considered as such. While every effort has been made to ensure the accuracy and reliability of the information, the author and publisher make no guarantees regarding its effectiveness for individual readers.

Readers are encouraged to consult with qualified professionals before making any decisions or changes related to health, finances, relationships, or other personal matters. The use of the strategies, techniques, and recommendations outlined in this book is at the reader's discretion, and the author and publisher assume no responsibility for any outcomes, positive or negative, resulting from their use.

By reading this book, you acknowledge that the author and publisher are not responsible for any decisions you make based on the information provided herein.

About the Author

Jayaa Mishra is a dedicated and passionate educator with extensive experience teaching both primary and secondary level students. Her commitment to continuous learning is evident as she actively engages with various coaches and mentors to enhance her knowledge and skills.

Ms. Jayaa Mishra has faced numerous challenges in her life, yet she has shown remarkable courage and resilience to overcome them. Her journey is a testament to the principles of courage and perseverance she has read about in books, proving them true through her own lived experiences.

MAY I ASK YOU FOR A SMALL FAVOR?

First, I want to thank you for reading this book. You could have chosen any other book, but you took mine, and I appreciate this. I hope you have at least a few actionable insights that will positively impact your daily life.

Can I ask for 30 seconds more of your time?

I'd love it if you could leave a review of the book. That will help me grow my readership by encouraging folks to take a chance on my books.

Keeping it straight - reviews are the lifeblood of any author.

It will take less than a minute of your time but will tremendously help me reach out to more people.

If you liked this book, please consider posting an honest review on your preferred retailer. And I'd love to see your review. Thanks for your support.